marie claire
Maison
SMALL SPACES

marie claire
Maison
SMALL SPACES

Hilary Mandleberg

First published in 2007 by
Quadrille Publishing Limited
Alhambra House,
27–31 Charing Cross Road,
London WC2H 0LS

Text © Hilary Mandleberg 2007
Photography © Photography © SIC 2007
Design and layout © Quadrille Publishing
Limited 2007

Editorial director: **Jane O'Shea**
Creative director: **Helen Lewis**
Editor and project manager: **Anne McDowall**
Art direction and design: **Lucy Gowans**
Production: **Vincent Smith, Bridget Fish**

British Library Cataloguing-in-Publication Data
A catalogue record for this book is available
from the British Library.

ISBN: 978 184400 505 5

Printed in China

Contents

Once upon a time, we all lived in small spaces. Primitive people dwelled in caves or huts in groups; farm workers lived in rural hovels with their animals, while the urban poor shared small, unsanitary rooms with their large families. Until the arrival of modern plumbing, most people lived in small multi-function spaces, keeping a chamber pot under the bed and washing in a bathtub in front of the kitchen fire. Possessions and clothing were minimal, so storage was not much of problem – a few hooks on the wall and a trunk in the corner, perhaps. Only the rich could afford the luxury of large-scale living.

Then, with the arrival of gas, electricity and sanitation, homes grew larger. As people became more affluent, they demanded more space and greater comfort, and house-builders strove to meet that demand. Now, ironically, at the start of the 21st century, we are returning to smaller homes. Space is once again a luxury, especially in urban areas, where many of us are living in spatially challenged homes out of necessity.

Others of us have decided to down-size because we are concerned about leaving too big an environmental footprint, while some of us choose to live small in an attempt to regain a life of simple values in an ever-more-complicated world. And then there are those of us who, having once bought into the loft-living dream, find we are uncomfortable in such large open spaces and have chosen instead to return to compartmentalised homes for the sense of reassurance and security that these smaller spaces bring.

Although currently you may be able to see only the problems posed by small-space living, there are plenty of positives too. Living small doesn't have to mean compromising

Right: *A sleek kitchen has been installed in the hallway of this compact space, where cooking, eating, working and relaxing all take place side by side. The shallow kitchen stands on a platform that conceals the plumbing. Although the kitchen area is decorated in a dark colour and the hallway is light, a sense of unity is maintained by the shelving, which gives the impression of running seamlessly between the two areas.*

Left: *This tiny apartment cleverly uses a number of ways of dividing the space into different zones. Sandblasted glass panels screen the bathing area from the kitchen and the bedroom from the living area without cutting out the light. A sofa and the headboard of the bed also form a divide between the bedroom and the living room. The final division, between the living and kitchen areas, is provided by a rosewood cabinet that opens to reveal kitchen appliances.*

on style or comfort. On the contrary, you may well find that you are able to afford a higher standard of finish and better quality fitments and furnishings than you could in a larger scale space simply because you will need less of them. And, because careful planning is of the essence in a small home, you should find that your space works super-efficiently.

Since many of us harbour the dream of spending less of our life commuting to and from work in the town or city, choosing to live in a small space may mean that you are able to live nearer to your place of work, which will benefit you mentally and emotionally as well as economically.

Editing your stuff so that is will fit into a smaller space can be hugely liberating. We sometimes find that our possessions have grown to the point where it feels as though they are taking over. If we could only ditch some of them, we tell ourselves, how much simpler life would be! If you are a hoarder, that argument may not chime with you, but don't forget that, thanks to modern technology, where you once needed a stereo system, countless LPs or CDs, photo albums and a small library of books, you can now store all that information and music in no more space than that taken up by a laptop or an iPod.

There are also lots of purely practical advantages to small-space living: a small space is easier to maintain than a large one, the running costs are lower and, as your lifestyle changes, it's not too difficult or expensive to tailor your small home to match. Finally, if none of these arguments has convinced you of the virtue of living small, heed the words of Leonardo da Vinci, who claimed that 'Small rooms or dwellings discipline the mind, large ones weaken it.'

1

EXPLORE YOUR SPACE

So how big exactly is your small space? Is it truly small – some people manage to make all the basic activities of life fit into as little as ten square metres – or is it simply not-so-big? The small spaces featured in this book range from a tiny eighteen square metres (see pages 84–5), to several with a relatively generous sixty square metres. How big is yours?

The next issue to consider is the number of people who live with you in your home. Clearly, what might work quite comfortably as a habitable space for one person – for example a small studio apartment where all the activities of living take place in one room – would be hopelessly inadequate for a couple or a family.

Then again, your small-space problem may have less to do with the size of the overall footprint of your house or apartment than with the need for an extra room – perhaps to accommodate a home office, a second bathroom or a guest bedroom. Or perhaps you are simply looking to find more storage space.

Maybe it's an individual room in your home that is the problem. Are you having trouble fitting all you need into that apparently small bedroom or bathroom? Or are you trying to make one room into a multi-function room? Perhaps you need a bedroom to double up as an office, or a kitchen to serve also as an eating area. At the other end of the multi-purpose scale is the loft space or studio apartment that you need to divide into smaller zones for different functions – living, eating, cooking, sleeping, bathing. How do you make those divisions work so that each activity has sufficient space?

Of course, if your small space is a second or holiday home, what you require from it may well be different. Many of us regard 'living small' as one of the delights of being on holiday, which accounts in part for the attraction of caravan and sailing holidays. If living small appeals to you, you will probably be prepared to put up with a tiny wet room instead of a bathroom, and a basic kitchen instead of a luxury one with all the latest appliances. You might even be content to have a shower in the corner of the kitchen like the owners of the weekend retreat on pages 24–5.

Opposite: *Space restrictions melt away when one looks out through this window at the view of the river. If you have a view, make the most of it either by enlarging the window, if you can, or by making sure that, when you use the space, the view takes centre stage. This tiny area in a 40-metre-square apartment serves both as office and dining room.*

What Do You Need From Your Space?

Faced with a small space that needs to be made liveable, you will want to think carefully about your priorities, and you will need to be prepared to compromise, especially if other people share your home. Drawing up a list of your absolute must-haves is a good place to start.

At the top of the list, of course, you should include the basics – areas in which to sleep, bathe, cook and sit. Some of these functions will need to occupy larger areas than others, but flexibility is possible. If you love cooking and entertaining, for instance, you will want a decent-sized, well-equipped kitchen with plenty of storage space, but to have that you may have to sacrifice a bit of space elsewhere, perhaps by having a small bathroom. On the other hand, you may be someone who lives on takeaways, in which case a mini kitchen is all you need and you may then have room for a more spacious living/entertaining area or a relatively spacious spa-type bathroom. Likewise, if your small space is a holiday home, a micro-kitchen that frees you from the tyranny of cooking may be just what you're after.

If you are one of the growing number of people who choose to work from home, having space for a work area will be a priority. Consider how large it needs to be to accommodate all the paraphernalia associated with your work. Could it be located in a living or sleeping zone, or even in a cupboard?

But living isn't just about eating, sleeping, bathing and working, it's also about relaxation, and with that comes the inevitable clutter of the stuff that we acquire – books, CDs, DVDs, sports gear, computer equipment, and so on. And for this you need lots of storage – a high priority in any small space.

PLANNING AHEAD AND BUDGETING

It's also important to think about how long you plan to live in the space. Is it a weekend retreat, your home for just a year or so, or do you intend to live there long term? And are you planning any lifestyle changes in the next few years that will affect the way you use the space? If you're wanting to start a family, for instance, you will need to think about how you can accommodate a new small person in your small space.

Finally, but very importantly, consider your budget. What funds you have available will inevitably affect what you can do to change your small space. But remember that you can always do things in stages. Start with what you can achieve without any major structural changes (see pages 16–23), and meanwhile start saving for that more costly extension or conversion.

Above: *This apartment has a second floor for a tiny bathroom, but the rest of the space has been cleverly configured to offer all the remaining essentials. The living area is not large, but good natural light and generously sized furniture make it seem bigger than it is.*

Opposite: *Although it is very compact, this kitchen packs in enough to make it easily adequate for a couple who enjoy cooking and entertaining.*

Working With What You've Got

If you live in rented accommodation, if you aren't planning to stay long in your small space, if it is a holiday home and you therefore don't want to spend a lot of money on it, or if you are simply a bit short of cash, it may be better to work with what you have in the way of space rather than build on to your property, make internal structural changes, or convert an area such as a loft or basement into a habitable room (see pages 26–39).

Fortunately, there are a surprising number of ways in which you can visually 'expand' and improve your small space that don't require the expenditure of vast amounts of cash. Indeed, in at least one case, you won't have to spend any money at all!

CUT THE CLUTTER

The most obvious thing you can do is to reassess all your possessions and decide if you really need them all. Getting rid of things can be painful, but it can be cathartic, too. Many of us have clothes stashed away that we haven't worn for years, books we read decades ago that we are unlikely to want to read again, stacks of old magazines lying around, household fittings or ornaments we have put to one side thinking we might use them again – one day.

You may even be one of those people who moved house years ago and haven't yet unpacked all the boxes! If you are, you could probably throw the boxes away and never miss their contents. Succeed in cutting some of the clutter and you may well find that many of your storage problems are solved and your home suddenly looks a whole lot bigger.

USING EVERY BIT OF SPACE

The next thing is to ensure that you are making the best use of all the space you have. This is important wherever you live, but in a small home, in particular, you need to make every nook and cranny work hard for you. Look around carefully and you might find there are many 'dead' spaces that you can use.

Perhaps you have a small alcove that is simply too tiny for storage, for instance. How about putting a radiator there, which might free up an area of more useable wall space elsewhere for a large storage unit? If you have a pair of alcoves on either side of a chimney breast – a common feature in older properties – they can easily be used for shelving or cupboards, or they might even accommodate a home office. For best effect, you should treat a pair of

Opposite: *A simple wet room screened by sandblasted glass and tiled entirely in small mosaic tiles gives an illusion of space, while a compact, metal washbasin reflects what light there is.*

Below: *This tiny triangular space manages to accommodate a washbasin, hand-held shower, towel hook and some shelves. In a shower space as small as this, it pays to use a hand-held shower.*

alcoves in the same way, whether that is by fixing shelving in both, building in cupboards, or with a mixture of the two – a cupboard below and shelving above. Another, inexpensive solution for a single alcove would be to screen it with a curtain and use it with a hanging rail and/or shelves for clothes storage, or as a way to conceal your sound system.

Perhaps you are looking for somewhere to locate a freezer, washing machine or tumble dryer. Remember that these appliances do not have to be in the kitchen. Indeed, given the noise that a washing machine or tumble dryer can make, it is often better not to locate them there anyway. For practical reasons, a freezer should be fairly close to the kitchen, but you may be able to stand it in a passageway outside the kitchen or perhaps under the stairs.

That understairs area might also serve as a good place to locate the washing machine or tumble dryer. Of course, you will need to ensure that you have the correct plumbing and drainage in place for a washing machine, while for a tumble dryer, you will need to be able to vent the damp air outside, or

buy a condensing model, which needs no vent. Making the necessary changes could prove expensive, but the cost may be worth it if you are able to liberate some valuable space elsewhere in the house as a result.

But before you try and find somewhere to locate these bulky appliances, have you first considered the possibility of managing with a combined fridge/freezer? Admittedly, this offers a smaller storage capacity, but it does have the advantage of taking up the floor space of only one machine. Likewise, if you need a tumble dryer, you may want to consider buying a washer/dryer that combines both functions in one machine. If that doesn't suit your lifestyle – and it may not if you have family wash loads to contend with – think about a pair of machines that stack one on top of the other. Again, both these options will free up floor space. And if you have somewhere to hang washing outside, why not do without a tumble dryer altogether, which could give you some useful wall space for shelving or a cupboard above the washing machine?

Opposite: *Here a bed has been fitted beneath the metal-ribbed curved ceiling of a former industrial space. Separated from the main area by a pair of floor-to-ceiling sliding doors, the bed is given a sense of enclosure and cosiness by the screen/headboard behind. Lighting at floor level is softly diffused through the space to help counteract the industrial feel of the architecture.*

MINI ROOMS FOR MINI AREAS

Some activities may not need entire rooms but could be accommodated in an area of otherwise dead space. Take the example of a home office. If all you need is a place to do your household accounts once a month, try fitting a small table and foldaway chair in the space under your stairs. Some good lighting, a power point for the computer and some file boxes might be all the extras needed to make this space work. Alternatively, you could use the space for a compact sofa.

Even the dead space in front of a window has its possibilities – and it will benefit from the natural light as well. Again, it could become a mini home office or other work area, or you could build in a window seat with storage beneath, that will offer a comfortable place for you to perch and enjoy the view.

Corridors can also become more than just linking spaces between rooms or areas: think about how you could incorporate built-in cupboards or shelving. (If you are able to make major changes – see pages 26–39 – you may even try using one for a bathroom. You need only enough room for the bath itself and for you to stand when you emerge from the tub, particularly if you fit a space-saving sliding door. Similarly, you could fit a wet room or toilet into a long narrow corridor space.)

Perhaps you want another bedroom. The basics of a bedroom are nothing more than a place to sleep and, ideally, somewhere to store clothes. If there is a corner of your home that could be closed off to contain a bed, you might be able to provide some clothes storage nearby, perhaps in the form of a floor-to-ceiling cupboard in a passageway. Of course, if you want a bedroom for just occasional use, a foldaway bed in a living room might do.

CHECKLIST: SIMPLE DEAD-SPACE SOLUTIONS

Alcoves
- Move a radiator to an alcove to free up wall space elsewhere
- Fit with shelving or cupboards or a combination of the two
- Turn into a home office
- Insert a hanging rail and screen with a curtain or door to use for clothes storage
- Use to conceal your sound system behind a curtain

Passageways and corridors
- Use as a home for appliances
- Install cupboards or shelving

Understairs area
- Use for appliances
- Turn into a mini office
- Create a seating area
- Make a children's play area

In front of a window
- Use as a mini office or other work area
- Add a window seat with storage beneath

Left: *There is a lot going on in this multi-function space. In the foreground, the living area is divided from the kitchen by a storage wall that doesn't quite reach the ceiling, which makes the space feel less enclosed and thus larger. On the other side of the wall is shelving for kitchen utensils, glassware and crockery. Beyond the kitchen, near the doors into the apartment, is an office, where a desk doubles as a dining table.*

MAKE A ROOM DO DOUBLE DUTY

If the dead spaces around your home cannot provide for the activity areas you need, think about whether, and how, you might double up the functions of existing rooms. For example, you may need a room for eating in, but do you really need a separate dining room, or might an eating area in the kitchen suffice? (Bear in mind that not many people have the luxury of a dining room nowadays, and those that do often find that it stands unused most of the time, except for special holidays and other family gatherings.)

If it is a home work space you are looking for, consider using your bedroom as an office during the day. If your bedroom is small, you could even install a foldaway bed and add a small filing cabinet that could double as a bedside table. Many manufacturers now make furniture and fittings that are less room-specific than they once were, which makes it easier to choose elements that will work equally well in either a bedroom or an office.

Of course, you may not relish the idea of facing your work station as soon as you wake up in the morning, in which case, try putting the office, rather than the bed, in a cupboard, perhaps as part of a wall of built-in storage. Such an arrangement will make it easier for you to segregate working and sleeping. If your work clutter really is too space-consuming to fit in a cupboard, then at least try to find a screen to hide it all away.

If you want an en-suite bathroom but don't have an adjacent room that you could use, consider putting a bathing area in the bedroom. Gone are the days of ugly shower enclosures: today's beautiful frame-free fitments will make a stunning focal point in any room, and some shower pods can even be built into a run of cupboards.

WAYS TO MAKE A SPACE FEEL BIGGER

• Choose space-saving, mobile or dual-purpose furniture wherever possible (see pages 136–53).

• Put your TV on a wall bracket, or have a plasma screen that lies flat on the wall, and keep the tabletop free for something else.

• Keep clutter tidied away out of sight and use pinboards for notes, letters and messages instead of leaving all those bits and pieces lying around.

• Rethink your lighting (see pages 120–3) and/or devote more wall space to mirrors or other reflective surfaces (see pages 126–9).

• Choose light-enhancing colours to decorate the space (see page 106–111).

• Use low-level furniture to keep sightlines free so that you don't feel closed in.

• Consider using sofas and chairs with legs rather than those that come right down to the floor. Being able to see the floor beneath them will give the illusion of more space.

• Avoid furniture with fussy detail and trims. The best has straight or gently curving lines.

• Underlighting bulky furniture, such as beds and built-in storage, will prevent it from looking so heavy.

CASE STUDY

A Weekend Hideaway

When your small space is a second home, it is easier to put up with a simple way of life. After all, part of the joy of going away for a weekend is the chance to get away from it all. This tiny hideaway started as nothing more than an ancient stone-built country cottage on a sloping site. It was slowly crumbling into a state of disrepair, but it has been transformed by its new owners. As well as restoring the stonework, they inserted new doors and windows, installed plumbing and a mezzanine and laid new concrete floors. Where there was an old well there is now a toilet, and a hot-water tank has been located beneath the outside staircase.

Despite the many improvements they have made, the owners have remained true to the building's humble origins. They have used rustic-style ironwork, simple country furniture and a muted, natural colour scheme throughout, and instead of smart new floors in the kitchen and living room, the builder laid grey concrete, then, while it was still wet, poured over white concrete and roughly mixed it in to create an attractive softly speckled effect.

Above: *The arched living room on the ground floor is furnished with garden chairs and second-hand furniture. Small niches have been carved out of the walls, which are finished with a mixture of chalk and local sand.*

Top: *The first-floor bedroom, decorated with the utmost simplicity, opens onto the terrace. A ladder leads up to a tiny mezzanine with a rough wood floor and spare bed.*

Centre: *Everything about the kitchen has a rustic feel, from the stone sink to the splashback made of old tiles. The wall light was originally an old grain scoop.*

Above left: *Because of the lack of space, the shower is located in a corner of the kitchen. It is screened by a linen curtain hanging from a piece of driftwood.*

Above: *The new doors and windows in this tiny renovation have been arranged to benefit from the views and to allow light right through the space.*

Changing What You've Got

If you have exhausted the possibilities of what you can achieve with your small space as it stands, it might be time to think about making alterations to improve, and possibly even extend, it. By making structural changes to your property, you can make the space work better by opening it up visually – it goes without saying that a closed-in area looks and feels more cramped than one that is open – and you will also achieve a better flow of movement throughout. In addition, you can create better storage arrangements, which are key to getting the most out of a small space. If you are able to afford more major structural changes, you may even be able to add extra space by converting an unused area such as an attic or basement, or by building an extension.

EMPLOYING PROFESSIONALS

If you are considering major structural changes to your property, you will certainly need to hire some professional help. Architects are specially trained to be able to maximise your home's potential, often in ways you may never have considered. A good architect will discuss your requirements with you in detail and will then come up with ideas that are within your budget and meet any legal and planning requirements.

You can employ an architect simply to draw up plans for you, which should include a detailed written specification covering materials and finishes, and monitor the work through the various planning stages, or he or she could see the project through to its completion. In this project-manager capacity, the architect will hire and co-ordinate all the other specialists you might require,

such as structural engineers, surveyors and contractors; will source the materials and ensure that they are delivered at the right time; and will make sure that the work is completed on time and within budget. The architect may also include penalty clauses in your contract with the contractor in case this is not achieved.

If the work is less complicated in nature, and you have the time, you may want to act as your own project manager once your plans have passed the approval stage. To do this, you will need to have a clear idea of the order of work and be able to give a good brief to the contractor or builder. (You can use a builder rather than a contractor if the work is straightforward and does not require a number of specialist skills.) A contractor should shoulder the burden of keeping a watchful eye over the progress of the work, arrange delivery of materials, ensure there are workmen on site when they should be and co-ordinate everything for you.

You may also want to consider enlisting the help of an interior designer or a specialist design service to help you choose your interior finishes – paint, wallpaper, lighting and flooring. Although this will involve an additional expense, these professionals can often make savings that they pass on to you when they buy what you need.

If you are planning a new kitchen or bathroom or are having a room fitted out with built-in storage, your specialist manufacturer will often offer a design and installation service as well. Such companies are generally able to provide a better installation service than a contractor or builder and they will also co-ordinate the arrival of everything you need, such as units, work surfaces, appliances and taps.

Opposite: If you have a roof space, it makes sense to use it, though be aware of the costs involved and of any building regulations. This under-the-eaves room benefits from the attractively shaped roof structure. Leaving it open-sided connects it visually to the room below, while painting it in a contrasting colour ensures that it is a focal point.

CHECKLIST: PROFESSIONALS AND WHAT THEY DO

● **Architect**
Has knowledge of planning and legal constraints; offers creative solutions; can either draw up plans, give written specification covering materials and finishes and see the plans through the planning process, or can act as project manager and oversee the project through from start to completion, ensuring it is completed on time and within the agreed budget.

● **Structural engineer**
Converts an architect's vision into functional reality by ensuring the safety of the finished structure.

● **Surveyor**
Assesses the suitability of the land and/or the structure of the building for the proposed work.

● **Building contractor**
Needs to be briefed either by you or by the architect; employs people with specialist skills as necessary; arranges delivery of materials; co-ordinates workmen.

● **Builder**
Employed for less complicated projects; needs to be briefed either by you or by the architect.

● **Interior designer**
Helps you choose interior finishes; can make savings on materials that they pass on to you when they buy what you need.

● **Specialist kitchen or bathroom supplier**
Provides room-specific design and installation service.

PLANNING AND LEGALITIES

Whether or not you need to seek planning permission for the work you intend to do will depend on the scale of the project and where you live. Make sure you check local planning requirements before you begin, and if your home is of historical or architectural importance, you may also need special permission to carry out work on it, even if the results are not visible from the outside.

Building regulations cover such issues as fire safety, sound insulation, drainage, ventilation and electrical safety. Failure to comply with building regulations may mean that you have to dismantle the work you have done.

You may also want to ensure that you choose environmentally friendly materials and consider the energy efficiency of your space.

SERVICES

Before you embark on a new building project, you will need to think about the services – heating, plumbing and electrics – you require. It makes sense, especially when space is limited, to fit as many of these services as possible behind the scenes to help achieve a streamlined look. This means building pipework and electrical conduits into walls and ceilings and under floors or, if that is not possible, into false walls or cupboards. Another option for electrical wiring is behind skirting boards. If you are planning to install a sound system, think about a complete floor-to-ceiling system that hides all the clutter, plugs and wires.

You can achieve a sleeker and less bitty look in a bathroom or kitchen – as well as saving on costs – if you locate all your services in the same run, for example placing the basin, bath and toilet in a row. If you live in, or are

Opposite:
Removing a wall between two rooms is a tried-and-tested way of gaining some space, but if you want to keep the two rooms separate while also increasing the sense of space, another option is to replace the wall with shelving that can be accessed from both sides. Here, the bookcase wall adds a sense of transparency.

planning to make, a multi-function space, grouping all the services into a single core is a space-saving and cost-effective solution. This will mean locating your kitchen and bathing areas adjacent to one another.

Boilers and radiators

These take up valuable wall space that could otherwise be used for those all-important cupboards and shelves. Fortunately, modern boilers are smaller and more efficient than they once were and there are also many space-saving models on the market. If finding somewhere to locate your boiler is a problem, consider spaces that might otherwise be wasted, such as under the stairs or high up on a wall. Don't forget, though, that you will need to vent the flue to the outside. Alternatively, you might be able to site a boiler in an adjoining garage.

Radiators now come in many guises and are more efficient, as well as better looking, than ever before. You may find that a small new radiator can produce as much heat as a larger old one, or that a tall, narrow, space-saving model will fit perfectly into a difficult corner of the room. Alternatively, move a radiator to a dead space such as above a toilet or in an alcove, or choose a long, low one that sits next to the skirting board or in a channel in the floor along the edge of a wall. These low-level options are far less visually obtrusive than the classic wall-hugging models.

Better still, replace radiators with ducted or warm-air heating or with underfloor heating. Ducted air heating systems are relatively rare, though popular in the USA, but you should be able to find a specialist firm to install it for you. Underfloor heating works especially well in a bathroom, and makes for a cosy floor when you're barefoot. Bear in mind, though, that underfloor heating doesn't suit some types of floor covering.

CHECKLIST: SPACE-SAVING SERVICES

Electrical wiring
Build into the wall
Build into the ceiling
Build into the skirting board
Build under the floor
Build behind false walls
Build into a cupboard

Plumbing
Locate in one run
Locate in single core
Build into the wall
Build into the ceiling
Build into the skirting board
Build under the floor
Build behind false walls
Build into a cupboard

Boiler
Choose a space-saving model
Locate under the stairs
Position high on a wall
Locate in the garage

Radiator
Choose a space-saving model
Locate in a 'dead' space
Choose a skirting-hugging model
Locate in a floor channel
Use underfloor heating instead
Use ducted air heating instead

Opposite: *In this room, a non-load-bearing wall was removed to open up the space so there was no need for a supporting beam or rolled steel joist to be inserted. The result is a combined dining/cooking area with an industrial feel.*

Opposite: *A panel of beige cotton has been pinned above this door opening and held back with a loop. Other simple options include walk-through bead, acrylic, wood, bamboo, shell or chain curtains.*

Below: *Here, a sandblasted glass door slides opens in front of a red-lacquered wall to reveal a 10-metre-square wet room that makes the entire 60-metre-square apartment seem much larger than it actually is.*

Unless your home is protected by planning restrictions (see page 28) or contains features of superb quality, you may want to remove fussy architectural details such as ceiling roses, cornices, picture rails and dado rails. Modern homes, unless they're neo-whatever, are usually free of such features, which were designed for an age of centre lights and a time when people pushed furniture back against the wall when it was not in use. Nowadays they serve only to break up walls and ceilings. Removing them will help to make a small space look more roomy.

Fireplaces, too, take up a lot of valuable space. Unless you have a beautiful one that you want to keep as a feature, you would be advised either to have it taken out completely, or to replace it with a sleek contemporary – and more efficient – model. If you have

a useable chimney, you may be able to have a real fire, or a wood-burning stove with glazed doors so that you can still enjoy seeing the flames.

DOORS

If you want to open up a small space consisting of a number of rooms, but don't want, or are unable, to take out walls, consider removing the doors between them. Although individual small rooms may have distinct personalities, they are likely to feel cramped. Removing doors will open up views into other parts of the home, which will make the space feel larger.

A hinged door takes up a surprising amount of space. If it is feasible to do so, try removing it altogether to leave just an opening. You might even be able to widen this entrance, or enlarge it so that it extends from floor to ceiling. If soundproofing isn't a particular issue and you want some way of separating two areas occasionally, you could use curtains as a screen.

If removing a door isn't feasible, for instance if you need privacy for a bathroom or bedroom, there are various other space-saving options you can consider. The most straightforward is simply to rehang a door so that it swings out of a small room instead of into it. Alternatively, consider replacing a hinged door with a space-saving sliding or concertina door. A sliding door can either lie flat against the wall when open or, better still, slide away completely into the wall cavity. This more sophisticated version has the advantage of leaving the adjacent wall space free. Finally, don't forget that you can enhance the passage of light through your small space by replacing a solid door with a glazed or semi-glazed door. And there are plenty of semi-opaque styles of glass to choose from where privacy is required.

WINDOWS AND GLASS

Just as removing doors or enlarging entrances can make your space feel bigger, so too can increasing the size of windows, adding extra windows or even glazing an entire wall (see page 36). Don't forget to consult an architect or structural engineer, though, to ensure that any work on structural walls is carried out safely. Creating a new window in an external or internal wall will enable you to 'steal' much-needed light from outdoors or from the next room and that will help to make your space feel lighter and more open.

You might, for instance, try replacing an existing window with a floor-to-ceiling window or with French or sliding doors. Another option is to insert one or more new windows high up on a wall. This is an ideal solution if you want to increase the amount of light entering a room but don't want to be overlooked.

If adding an opening window isn't an option, consider replacing a section of wall with glass bricks. Like semi-transparent sheet glass, glass bricks will allow light to enter but will preserve your privacy.

As for your new internal windows, there is no need to be boring and have rectangles. Internal windows can be any shape you desire – square, round, half-moon – and you can leave them open or have them glazed in whatever type of glass you like.

Roof windows

Another way of introducing light into your small space – often with even more dramatic effect – is to add a roof or dormer window or a skylight. Tilting or pivoting roof windows are commonly used in loft conversions. A dormer window – a gable projecting from a sloping roof with a vertical window in it – is another alternative. However, although a dormer will give you more space, it is more complicated structurally – and therefore also more expensive. A skylight is usually positioned in a flat roof, such as you might have in an extension.

Another way of bringing light into a room is via a tubular skylight. A clear dome on the roof channels natural light down through reflective tubing directly to where it's needed in the room below. Tubular skylights are relatively easy to install and all you see in the ceiling is a round window. The joy of skylights and of some of the tubular skylights is that they give you a view of the sky overhead. They are great positioned directly above a bathtub!

Glass floors

Another means of bringing light into a space – and one that would be sure to make your home a talking point – is to insert a panel of specially strengthened glass into the floor. You could even consider creating an entire glass floor. Again, you will need to consult a structural engineer for any work of this nature. A glass floor will allow light as well as views into lower rooms and is especially useful for a basement conversion (see page 38).

Remember, though, that anyone beneath you will have a clear view up. It is therefore advisable to choose translucent rather than clear glass. And for safety reasons, you should make sure that the glass you use is anti-slip as well as specially strengthened for the purpose.

Left: *A glass wall at mezzanine level makes this double bedroom feel much larger than it is by creating a link with the well-lit living room downstairs. Space-enhancing all-white decoration adds to the effect. If you plan to install an all-glass wall, use some marking device to warn people not to walk into it. Here, the window frames perform that function.*

Opposite: *In a small room created in a roof space, a roof window provides much-needed light. Although you may want to enjoy seeing the sky outside, bear in mind that, in a bedroom, unless you screen the window with a blind, you will have light entering in the early hours on summer mornings.*

engineer before attempting to remove a wall in case it is load-bearing – but the main drawback is that you will end up with fewer wall surfaces to use for cupboards and shelving.

If you don't want to remove a wall completely, there are some less radical options to consider. You could instead have a half-height or half-width wall (see page 48), either constructed like a traditional stud wall and finished in plaster or tiles, or made of structural glass or of glass bricks. Such a half-wall will open up the space but still give that sense of there being separate 'rooms' or zones.

Another possibility – and one that is becoming increasingly popular – is to replace an entire wall with structural glass. This will enable you to enjoy a sense of light and space while still retaining separate rooms.

REMOVING OR ADDING CEILINGS

Another major change you could make to your small space is to remove a ceiling and/or add a mezzanine level. If your room is under the eaves, removing the ceiling will make the room feel more spacious and open. Alternatively, if you are very short of space, you may decide to leave the ceiling in place and instead convert the under-the-eaves or attic space to make a whole new living area (see page 38). Either way, make sure that your roof is properly insulated or you will be faced with an enormous loss of heat and astronomical heating bills.

Removing a ceiling may also give you the opportunity to insert a mezzanine floor. Or, if your ceilings are high enough – as is often the case in older houses – you may be able to add a mezzanine without removing a ceiling first. In this case, though, you may find that the resulting head height limits

Above: *A solid bathroom wall has been replaced with translucent panels that allow the light through from the bathroom to the adjacent space. This solution suits a deep space that has windows along only one wall as it prevents interior areas from being dark and gloomy.*

REMOVING WALLS

Turning two or more rooms into one large single-use room or multi-purpose living area by removing a wall or walls is a tried-and-tested way of opening up a small space. Indeed, larger multi-function rooms began to be popular in the fifties and sixties as central heating became more widely available and enabled homeowners to dispose of their then-redundant fireplaces.

Opening up your space by removing a wall will help improve movement through your home and will make the space feel lighter and bigger. Clearly this is a costly undertaking – you'll need to consult a builder or structural

Above: *A floor-length curtain effectively screens this mezzanine bedroom from the* *rest of the loft space at night. The whole effect is comfortable and cosy, despite the limited space.*

you and you can use the new space only as a sleeping platform. (A roof window or skylight situated directly above the bed will help make the space feel less claustrophobic.) Though mezzanines are often used for bedrooms, they may be capable of providing some storage or home office space as well, and they may even house bathing facilities. For more on mezzanines, see pages 60–5.

CONVERSIONS

Having exhausted all the possibilities of creating more space from the rooms you already occupy, you may want to consider converting space that is currently unused, or that is used for something other than living – an attic, basement or garage, for example.

Unfortunately, such conversions are not cheap and you may not recoup your costs when you sell your home. Basements, for example, need thorough waterproofing before they can be made liveable and they may need digging out. And in order to have access to natural daylight, you will need to install a lightwell or glazed roof. An attic will need insulation, windows, strengthened joists and access via a staircase, while a garage will need insulation, windows and access from the house. In addition, you will need to allow for the supply of services, and for wall and floor finishes.

However, if the space is deemed to be suitable and your budget will stretch to it, you will end up with a whole new room that you can use for anything you wish – an extra living area, a second bathroom or guest bedroom, a home office or even a kitchen.

It is best to use one of the specialist companies that undertake such conversion work. Ask for recommendations to make sure you choose one that is reputable. A good company will not only draw up the plans for you but will also obtain all the permissions you require, will draw up a party-wall plan with your neighbour if needed, and will ensure that all building regulations are adhered to.

EXTENSIONS

If you have the room, and can get planning permission, an extension can be a cheaper option than moving home to get the space you need. As with any major building work, you should employ an architect and contractor, and you may want to think about using an interior designer, too. The best plans will not only provide you with your extra room, but should also integrate perfectly with the space you already have, including, if the extension is at ground level, with your garden.

Extending a kitchen into the garden space is a popular option. You can do this either by means of a conservatory (many styles can be bought off-the-peg, which can be cost-effective) or by building a single-storey extension to give you a kitchen/diner or simply a more spacious kitchen. If funds and planning permission allow, you might want to think about building a double-height extension, which would give you another extra level, too.

Building either an extension or a conservatory does have certain pitfalls, however. A single-storey extension that is not all glass can be dark, though you can counteract this by installing a large skylight and perhaps also glass doors that fold back on themselves. Your architect or designer will be able to advise you. A conservatory, though light, can overheat quickly when the sun shines and may be cold in winter. To make sure it is fit for purpose, install adequate heating for winter use, fit blinds to help keep it cool in summer, and consider using special solar-control glass to keep the heat at bay.

Opposite: *In this attic conversion, a floor bed is tucked beneath the curving roof, allowing just enough height for getting out of bed safely. The furniture around the bed is low too, which helps keep the sightlines clear and enhances the sense of space.*

2

THE MULTI-FUNCTION SPACE

Life these days is far less compartmentalised than it was a generation or so ago. This, plus the fact that many of us now have much smaller living spaces, means that open-plan, multi-function spaces are more in tune with the way we live now. No longer is a living room just for relaxing or entertaining; today we might just as often use it for eating and working.

A multi-function room – and the studio apartment or one-room living space represents the concept at its most extreme – can be a great solution for a home where space is at a premium, but there are, of course, disadvantages to this way of living. There is no escaping the fact that if the TV or the food processor is on, it will be heard all around the space – and you will also have to deal with the smells that waft from the kitchen area. There is also a lack of privacy, which is fine if you live alone, but not always acceptable if you share with others. Then there is the simple fact that one-space living gives you fewer walls against which to stand furniture.

One of the keys to successful open-plan living is to make sure that each function works efficiently in its own right. You can achieve this by ensuring that space is not wasted, that movement around the room follows a natural flow without any obstructions, and by locating in close proximity to one another areas of activity that are suited to being linked – cooking and eating, living and working, sleeping and bathing or sleeping and working, for example. Fortunately, today's furniture is far less room-specific than it once was, which means that it is relatively easy to find, for instance, a cupboard that is equally at home in the working or bedroom area, or a table that could be used either for dining or as a work surface.

For maximum flexibility, it is helpful if you can close off, partially or completely, functional areas of your space such as the work zone and kitchen. This will help to ensure that your living and sleeping areas remain relaxing places to escape to when you need to. Paradoxically, if you can define the various zones of your multi-function space so that the whole resembles a sequence of 'rooms' rather than one large space, this will not only make your home look more spacious, but will also help it function more successfully.

Opposite: *This room, once three, is now a single multi-function space, lit by a row of large windows all along one wall. Functions are delineated by the furniture, while the decorating scheme – white walls and a wood floor throughout – provide the unifying element.*

Screens and Partitions

The beauty of many partitions and screens is their versatility – the fact that they can be moved to reveal or conceal part of the space as required. If, when you've finished working at your desk, you can pull a screen across the area and go and relax in the living space, you will be able to switch off as easily as if you had left a separate office. Different types of screening offer varying degrees of privacy, flexibility, and light and sound exclusion. Consider the various options and weigh up what is important to you before deciding which type best suits your needs.

FREESTANDING SCREENS

The most simple way of dividing space is with a freestanding screen, usually made of several panels that you can close or open according to the area you want to screen. In the 18th, 19th and early 20th centuries, freestanding screens were often used as a way to avoid draughts in the days before central heating. Today, you could use one to delineate a zone and/or provide privacy, for example by screening a home office from a bedroom or living area, a dressing area from a bedroom,

Above: *An elaborate wrought-iron screen dressed with fabric is all that is needed to separate the sleeping area from the bathing area in this en-suite bedroom.*

or a bathing zone from a bedroom or from a window. You may be lucky enough to find an old screen in an antique shop. Alternatively, look for ready-made screens in contemporary materials and designs, or have one made to your own specifications.

Although freestanding screens are decorative, easy to move around and inexpensive compared with structural methods of dividing up a larger space (see pages 46–8), they do not offer a great deal of privacy and can feel rather flimsy.

CURTAINS AND HANGING PANELS

A curtain used across a door opening or an alcove is an inexpensive and easy way to divide one area from another. As well as the obvious fabric options, consider curtains made from attractive beads or lengths of chain. However, curtains will not give you much privacy from noise, nor, unless they are made of a thick material, will they screen light coming from another part of the space.

Left: *Voile curtains hanging from a pole suggest that the bed is screened from other areas of the home, but here the effect is more decorative than practical.*

Opposite: *When they are not in use, these semi-opaque floor-to-ceiling panels slide back on top of one another so that the bedroom remains half-screened from the living area and the volume of the whole space is not compromised.*

Lightweight panels hung from tracks fitted to the ceiling or near-ceiling level provide another versatile and relatively inexpensive screening option. One panel slides over the next, rather like a vertical blind, and when open, the panels either remain on show, stacked up together, or can be stowed away in a double-thickness wall.

Sliding panels work especially well to screen a bed from a living area, when they may resemble the drapes around a four-poster bed. These panels enable you to open up or screen off as much of an area as you choose, but like a freestanding screen, they do not offer much privacy, nor will they exclude light and sound. Sliding panels may be made of Perspex or glass – slightly more sound-proof – as well as of specially treated fabric. Floor-to-ceiling concertina panels that fold flat against a wall or that disappear into a double-thickness wall make a good alternative to sliding versions.

SOLID SLIDING PANELS

Solid sliding panels and entire sliding walls that run along a track provide a very versatile solution to the problem of dividing up a larger space into smaller zones. They also offer far greater privacy and potentially better sound- and light-proofing, depending on their material and construction. But they are, of course, more expensive than most other types of screening.

Capable of completely transforming an open-plan space into one composed of separate, though flexible, 'rooms', sliding panels work well as a division between a sleeping area and a living, working or bathing zone. Depending on whether you want the partial division provided by a panel or the more solid effect of a wall, materials can be lightweight or more substantial, but whichever you choose, opt for a clean, streamlined finish, with flush handles (if handles are needed).

Above: *In this space, two of a trio of freestanding walls end below ceiling height and the third – the wall that screens the bathroom – is topped by a glass panel to provide extra privacy. Access either side of the walls, and a sense of space above them, ensures that the room does not feel at all cramped.*

HALF-WALLS

Half-walls – half-height or half-width – are structural features, and are therefore more costly, as well as less versatile, than screens. But because they don't impede the views through a space as a full-size wall does, they divide it without making you feel hemmed in. Like curtains and sliding screens, though, half-walls don't offer much in the way of sound exclusion.

For a hardly-there look, have a half-height or half-width wall constructed as a stud wall and finish it to blend with the walls of your room. For less obstruction of the light, and for an even greater sense of spaciousness, choose glass – clear or translucent or glass brick – or Perspex.

A half-height wall makes an effective divide between a kitchen and a living area, where it will conceal cooking clutter from view. A half-width wall can be used to screen a toilet from the rest of the bathroom. Here, where you may not need a solid wall, consider using glass bricks or a translucent glass panel. Either would preserve your modesty while still allowing light to pass through from the main space. This sort of wall is also useful for dividing a bathroom from a bedroom. Keeping the space partially open between the adjacent rooms with a translucent glass wall rather than a solid one will make both rooms feel larger and more luxurious.

The designer of the apartment on pages 50–1 has even put a fireplace in the half-width wall that divides the living area from the bathroom, making the partition a great focal point as well as giving it a double function. Alternatively, you could fit out a half-width wall with shelves for storage, or insert a TV screen or sound system.

If you want to create a more substantial division between zones, consider a partition wall that almost reaches the ceiling. Leaving a gap between the top of the partition and the ceiling will help to maintain a feeling of flexibility and space, while still ensuring that the screened-off area feels like a proper room. This is also a good solution if light and sound exclusion are important, as well as for areas where you may want more privacy, for example between a bedroom and a bathing or dressing area.

Finally, remember that a half-width wall doesn't need to be straight. It can be a rhomboid shape or can have a wavy edge. A half-wall that almost reaches the ceiling can even be circular or snail-shaped to provide a screen for a shower and, in a larger configuration, can screen off an entire bathroom from the bedroom (see page 66).

CHECKLIST: CHOOSING HOW TO SCREEN

Freestanding screens
- Available in many styles, sizes and materials
- Relatively inexpensive
- Do not provide much privacy
- Do not protect from light and sound

Curtains
- Provide a simple and inexpensive screening solution
- Available in many materials
- Do not provide much privacy
- Do not shield from light unless very thick

Sliding lightweight panels
- Versatile and relatively inexpensive
- Enable you to open up or screen off as much as you choose
- Do not provide much privacy
- Do not protect from light and sound

Solid sliding panels
- More expensive than most other options
- Provide a far greater degree of privacy
- Can provide reasonable sound- and light-proofing
- Enable you to open up or screen off as much as you choose
- Create a real sense of a room division

Half-walls
- More expensive than other options
- Divide space without making you feel hemmed in
- Do not provide a soundproof barrier
- As they are structural, may be used as more than just a way of dividing space

Above: *This pretty freestanding screen has been used to temporarily divide off the area of the room that is being used for doing the ironing. When it is no longer needed for that purpose, it is a decorative object in its own right or can easily be moved elsewhere.*

MAKE IT WORK FOR YOU

Screens and Partitions

In this loft apartment converted from an industrial space, all the windows are situated along one wall. The owner wanted to ensure that as much natural light as possible would be available in every 'room', no matter how far from the windows, so decided to use a mixture of glass, tailor-made translucent panels set in metal frames, metal frames without any infill, and a stud-wall partition.

Glass is used between the kitchen and the bedroom, ensuring that as much light as possible flows through. Pivoting polycarbonate screens, which provide more privacy than glass, divide the bedroom and the living area; these can be completely closed thanks to cupboard magnets in the ceiling covered with a thin layer of plaster to help disguise them. The bathroom is almost totally enclosed by solid stud walls. Metal frames without screening top one of these stud walls, creating the impression of there being another room at a higher level, but this is just an illusion.

Opposite: *One side of this converted industrial space consists of a series of small 'rooms' that are either half open or capable of being completely closed off. From left to right are a kitchen, bedroom and, behind the fireplace, a bathroom. The area in the foreground is left open as the living and dining space.*

 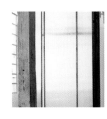   

Stud-wall partition
If you have space, it can pay to combine more than one type of partition to suit different purposes. Here, a half-wall of stud construction provides the necessary degree of seclusion to screen the bathroom.

Translucent partition
A partition made of polycarbonate provides an effective pivoting screen without blocking out light. Glass blocks achieve a similar effect but take up more floor space and remain fixed in position.

Focal point
Try turning a half-width stud wall into a focal point. You could use it for a fireplace, as here, for a flatscreen TV, to display a piece of artwork or for bookshelves. You could even paint it a dramatic colour or paper it.

Structural elements
If you are lucky enough to have attractive structural elements such as old wooden wall and ceiling beams, consider exposing them to add character to a room and to emphasise the different zones.

Low furniture
Although this room benefits from plenty of height and doesn't necessarily need low furniture, its use underlines the sense of space and allows the eye to focus on the decorative effect of the metal framing of doors and walls.

Furniture and Fittings

Every room needs its furniture and fittings, so why not make yours work twice as hard by using it to demarcate the different zones in your multi-function living space? If you can't find something appropriate off the peg, then consider having a piece of furniture or a fitting designed and built to suit your needs. Although this is a more expensive option, the positive effect it has on your space may make it well worth the extra cost. Demarcating zones in this way works best when you need to divide a living space from a dining area, home office or kitchen, or a sleeping zone from an adjacent bathing area or office space.

TALL DIVISIONS

Where you require a greater degree of privacy or a more definite division, the taller the fitting or piece of furniture the better. Tall dividers are especially useful for screening off a sleeping area. For example, a tall deep cupboard could provide wardrobe space in a bedroom but conceal the bathroom (see above). You might even be able to attach a basin or shower to it on the other side. Or a tall cupboard might form a super-sized headboard on the bedroom side. Like an island unit (see page 53), you can walk around it completely, so it helps to make the

Above: *This freestanding wardrobe not only provides essential storage space but also acts like a wall to divide a bedroom from its en-suite bathroom.*

'rooms' on both sides feel larger, yet its height gives the privacy you require.

If privacy isn't such an issue, you might be happy to have a lower headboard/divider like the one shown above. Such a headboard can be designed to incorporate storage if you wish, either in the form of shelving within the thickness of the headboard or as by-the-head storage in its width.

Another tall dividing option is to use a huge bookcase as a freestanding unit. If you want maximum flexibility, fit it with sturdy, lockable wheels so you can move it around. If the unit is open, so that its contents can be accessed from both sides, it will not only be more versatile, but will also help to maintain a sense of space (see page 87).

If your multi-function space is on two levels, it might be possible to position the stairs in such a way that they form a divide between one or more zones. You could also incorporate some storage underneath, though this will give you a less open look than would an open-tread staircase.

KITCHEN/LIVING ROOMS

Island units are a perfect way to divide a kitchen and living area. Depending on its length, such a unit might incorporate a hob, a sink, some storage and/or a worksurface. The advantage of an island unit is that it allows a free flow of traffic around it, which will help make your small space feel more roomy. And, of course, you will be able to work in your kitchen while chatting to people in the living zone. For maximum versatility,

Above: *Here, furniture is used to create zones in a multi-function room. Low-backed chairs help ensure that sightlines are kept free and that the space retains a feeling of openness.*

attach lockable castors to the unit (see pages 146–7) so that you can move it around as you please and have a handy work surface wherever you need it. (Castors are unsuitable for a unit containing a hob or sink, which need to remain attached to services.)

Instead of stopping a row of base units short where the kitchen meets the living area, have the base units turn a right-angled corner and continue across to form the divide. This arrangement has the bonus of giving you some more kitchen storage space as well as extra work surface. If you are using the unit to separate the kitchen from a dining area, you might want to fit the doors on the dining side and use the storage space for crockery and glassware.

FURNITURE DIVIDERS

Not all space-dividing furniture has to be on a large scale. A long sofa, a row of squashy floor cushions or nothing more than a couple of small chairs will do the trick, as might a big L-shaped sofa, one arm of which acts as the space divider. To maintain a sense of space while demarcating zones, it is best to use low-level furniture, though a pair of high-backed armchairs can be effective, too. These defy the 'rule' because there's some space between the two chairs, which helps visually and psychologically to lessen their bulk.

Other low-level pieces of furniture that work well to divide a space include the sideboard and other low storage units such as bookcases and stereo equipment storage units. Tables can work well, too. A long, tall console table makes a good choice, as does any long table, perhaps one that doubles up as a dining table and desk.

In a bedroom that is also an office, try using a row of filing cabinets to divide the space, although avoid the sort that come from an office supply company unless you like industrial chic. Another idea is a low storage unit or chest at the foot of the bed. Although this won't actually hide your work zone from view at bedtime, it will create a form of psychological barrier.

If you love plants, consider using a row of tall, matching planters to divide up a multi-function space, or try taking the idea a stage further and build the planting area into the floor.

BLURRING THE BOUNDARIES

In small spaces, especially, creating very obvious divisions between zones isn't necessarily the best solution. A more subtle approach involves blurring the boundaries. For example, you might extend a piece of furniture such as a kitchen worktop or a long desk into the adjoining living space. Since you don't then know where the kitchen or office ends and the living space begins, both spaces will feel much bigger.

Left: *In this small space, a kitchen base unit and the upstand behind it divide the kitchen from the bathroom, where a shower and toilet are concealed behind the half-wall seen in the background.*

Opposite: *This view shows how the division works from the bathroom side. The decorating scheme unites the two rooms: the same materials are used for the upstands and work surfaces in both, and the extractor fan/lighting panel runs the length of the wall.*

Change of Flooring

You may think that, unless you're going barefoot, you don't really notice what sort of flooring you're walking on. However, subconsciously you do, so use this knowledge and make a change of flooring in your multi-function space help to signify a change of zone. As when you use a low-level piece of furniture to divide a space, or use a change of colour scheme, an area of different flooring suggests a change of zone while still maintaining the sense of an open-plan space.

For practical reasons, you will no doubt want to vary the flooring in different areas anyway. Unless you live in a hot climate, you won't want to put your bare feet on the same flooring as you'd have in a bathing area, nor would you want to have a carpeted floor getting messed up in the kitchen.

In a multi-function space, try using a large rug for your living or sleeping area and go for hard flooring – wood, stone, ceramic, poured concrete, linoleum or rubber – for the places where this is most practical, for instance the kitchen or bathroom zone.

But what if your small space is truly tiny? While it is true that flooring takes up a significant area and is a great unifier of space, you can still use a change in surface to demarcate different zones without it making the space seem even smaller. The solution is to stick to a unified, light-toned colour scheme. Choose a pale neutral with lots of white in it to reflect the light – off-white, beige or grey, for instance – and choose your different flooring materials from within the same colour range. Your subconscious will be aware of the change of flooring as you move around the space, and the textural contrasts inherent in the different materials will help as well.

If you are lucky enough to have a multi-function space that is somewhat larger, you can probably get away with laying a boldly coloured kelim or contemporary rug in front of the sofa. Just make sure that you keep some neutral flooring around it so that it floats in the space instead of dominating it, and limit the colour and pattern you use elsewhere.

And if your space allows, you might like to try the 'blurring-the-boundaries' trick (see page 54) with your flooring as well. Instead of stopping the kitchen flooring exactly at the line where the living area starts, or the bathroom flooring where the bedroom begins, allow it to flow over into the next zone. This will baffle you into thinking that both areas are larger than they really are.

Opposite: *The change from shiny white sheet flooring to wooden flooring marks the move from kitchen to dining area, though the distinction between the two is blurred by the long counter top/table that links the spaces.*

Below left: *Here, the clear division between a hallway and adjoining kitchen is marked by the change of flooring from wood to ceramic tile.*

Change of Colour Scheme

Just as a switch from one type of flooring to another in a multi-function space sends a message to the brain that there's some change going on in the space you're moving around in, so a change in colour scheme can signal that you're walking from one zone into another. A change of colour scheme can also help to simplify and clarify the visual logic of a large multi-function room, while a lack of contrast can make the space feel barren or chaotic.

This does not mean using 'Toy Town' colour scheming – decorating the living area blue, an adjacent work zone yellow and the kitchen next to that red, for example. If you did that, the result would be bitty and disturbing and the effect as you look or move from one zone to another will be uncomfortable and awkward. Instead, you need to find a decorating scheme that uses subtle shifts and changes of emphasis that maintain a sense of unity while defining the different zones.

SUBTLE CONTRASTS

One way to achieve this is to use a colour scheme that offers some gentle contrasts from area to area. Each colour should be discernibly different from its neighbour but not to the extent that the colours jar. Paint charts are a good place to start: pick a colour, then choose other colours from those that surround it on the chart. These are generally all tints (the core colour with varying degrees of white added) and shades (the base colour plus varying degrees of black) of the same colour, which means that they look good together but also offer enough of a contrast to achieve the desired effect. Try applying this approach to colour scheming to the various zones of your space, using the core colour in one area, a tint in another and a shade somewhere else. For even greater subtlety, try the core colour in, say, the living area, and use a shade of that core colour for your seating, then repeat the shade for a wall of the cooking zone. You will sense the slight shifts as you move around in the space.

ACCENTING

Another option is to use a lighter or darker accent colour to draw attention to a particular architectural feature of the room. Try painting a run of storage units in a kitchen zone in a boldly contrasting colour so that they stand out from the more neutral colours of the living zone, or use a light contrast colour on the front of a half-wall to help emphasise the move from one area of the room to another.

Try grouping sofas and chairs around a colourful rug in the living area and use a colour from the rug to paint a kitchen wall, or pick up on it in a collection of dining chairs. Or surround your sleeping zone with built-in storage finished in a certain colour and echo that colour in the accessories in the bathroom. By using colour in this way, you will both unite the various zones of your space and define each one visually.

Another option is to choose three harmonising but distinct colours from a colour chart and repeat and mirror them throughout the multi-function space in different proportions, for example using a bit more of a light colour in one zone and going for more of a dark one elsewhere.

Opposite: *A dramatic change of colour scheme from light to dark changes the mood entirely between a bedroom and its en-suite bathroom. However, the white of the bedroom is echoed in the bathroom basin and light fitting, while the mainly black scheme of the bathroom is mirrored in the dark bedspread and bedside table of the sleeping area.*

Change of Level

Introducing a change of level in your multi-function space is a more complex undertaking from the structural point of view, but it can bring great rewards. A variation of level in any room is an interesting and unusual feature, but in a multi-function room it can help signal a change of function, too.

A SMALL STEP

Raising the level of the floor by even just fifteen or twenty centimetres is the simplest option. For example, you could create a low sleeping platform with storage beneath (see opposite), or a seating area with the same.

If you would like to go for a change of level on a slightly bigger scale, consider raising the floor beneath a larger part of your multi-function room. A kitchen area lends itself especially well to this treatment because the utilitarian functions of a kitchen are so distinct from those of the rest of a living space. That step up to reach your kitchen will provide it with extra definition and a great sense of demarcation – but for safety reasons, it's a good idea to highlight the step.

You could, if you wished, underline the change by treating the raised area to different flooring (see pages 56–7), and a change of lighting will help too. (A kitchen will in any case require a different lighting treatment.) However, make sure that it is clear visually that the raised area is still part of the same larger space. You can do this by linking the decorative scheme in some way – by painting walls or cupboard fronts in the same colour in the different areas, for example, or by using accessories that echo one another across the various zones.

MEZZANINES

More dramatic still is to build a mezzanine into your multi-function space. This is a complex structural undertaking that needs careful planning and design. It may, for example, require additional support for the new floor. It is obviously easier to fit in a mezzanine if you have a tall or, better-still, double-height room. If you don't, maybe you have access to the roof space above and could remove the ceiling to give you the height you need.

In a multi-function room with a very small floor area, a mezzanine makes a lot of sense as it provides a whole extra room and can look great, too. Remember, though, that the larger the floor area of the mezzanine, the less of the room below will be full-height and the less light there will be in that part of the room. This is something to bear in mind if the entire space is very small – you don't want to feel claustrophobic on both levels. Here, a sleeping platform may be the best option as this need be only a little larger than your mattress.

Even if your mezzanine is nothing more than a sleeping platform, however, it should ideally have enough headroom for you to be able to stand up. You can manage with less if you have to, but it's not ideal, except perhaps as an extra bedroom for occasional use. If headroom is lacking, you could install a skylight above the bed to give a sense of space.

Before you rush off to build a mezzanine, bear in mind that there may be no way of blocking the noise from the living area downstairs. This might be fine if you live on your own, but it's not so great if you live with others, particularly if you want to use the mezzanine for a bedroom.

Opposite: In a small multi-function room, even a minimal change of level can make a difference. Here, simply raising the bed on a platform in an alcove makes the sleeping area feel quite separate from the rest of the room. This simple device also offers the possibility of extra storage space in drawers beneath it.

Staircases

You also have to consider how you are going to reach your mezzanine. You will want to ensure that the staircase takes up as little room as possible – particularly if your entire space is tiny – both in terms of its width and its rake. A staircase with a steep rake will use up less of the space below, and a spiral staircase will take up less room than a normal staircase, but neither is a good choice for the young, the elderly or the infirm. If your staircase is leading only to a sleeping platform, you might be able to manage with nothing more than a ladder, just as for a child's bunk bed.

Though you can make the staircase into a focal point if you wish, it must be fit for purpose and must meet local building regulations, which might mean that a beautiful, hardly-there, steep and narrow staircase without a handrail is not an option.

Balustrades

How are you going to make sure that you don't fall off the mezzanine? A fully open platform can look wonderful, but it's not a good idea if you're a restless sleeper or if there are children around – and, again, it may not meet local building regulations. A safer alternative is to include some sort of balustrade. This could be either a stud wall with a normal plaster finish that's painted, or a balustrade made of metal, wood or even translucent structural glass.

Opposite and above: *Because this multi-function space had the benefit of height, the owner was able to add a mezzanine to use as a sleeping area. The staircase emerges at the back of the mezzanine so that it intrudes only minimally into the room below, and everything in the sleeping area is low level to help maximise the sense of space.*

MAKE IT WORK FOR YOU

Change of Level

One of the most efficient ways of configuring a space with a small floor area but a high ceiling is to install a mezzanine. That's exactly what the young Italian designer–owner of this 45-square-metre 'pod for living' did with the part of an old paper mill that he had bought. By adding a made-to-measure steel staircase that takes up the minimum of space, he now has – downstairs – a living area, dining 'room', kitchen and – hidden away behind what looks like a built-in cupboard – a bathroom, which even has room for a bidet. Upstairs, beneath the arched concrete ceiling, is his bedroom, with a generously sized office area.

Having already spent most of his budget on the structure of the mezzanine itself, he made the most of cheap, industrial materials, such as concrete for walls and floors and scaffolding planks for the mezzanine floor. Although briefly tempted by the idea of making his small space minimal, he instead decided to stamp his own style on it by using a quirky mix of off-the-peg furniture and fittings.

Opposite: *This hard-working split-level apartment proves that living in a small space can be efficient, comfortable and stylish. The addition of the mezzanine is key to the successful use of the space, but the clever choice of furnishing means there's never a sense of being cramped or overcrowded.*

Understairs storage
If your home is tiny, every bit of it must work hard, even the apparently dead space beneath the stairs. Good storage is a small-space essential, too. Here the two meet with great results.

Floor-to-ceiling doors
White laminate doors conceal not just cupboards but the bathroom, too. Although they divide the already small space, they cleverly suggests there's much more going on behind.

Mini-kitchen
With a space this small, you won't be cooking on a large scale, but you can still find room for kitchen basics. Look for handy all-in-one hob/sink/storage units and pair with shelves instead of wall cupboards.

A change of flooring
One way to make a small one-room-living space seem bigger is to divide it into 'rooms'. Here, the rug separates the living 'room' from the concrete-floored kitchen and dining 'room'.

Low-level seating
Low-level furniture adds a sense of spaciousness to a small room. Here, huge floor cushions provide the necessary seating and also help to define the different zones of the multi-function space.

Room within a Room

One of the cleverest ways of dividing up a multi-function space into smaller zones is to completely encase an area in walls to create a room within the main room. The walls don't have to be floor-to-ceiling, the area you enclose may be only the size of a large cupboard, and you may not even need doors to make it work. If you have sufficient headroom, you might be able to maximise the use of space even further by creating an upper level in your room within a room.

PURPOSE-BUILT ROOMS

In its largest incarnation, a room within a room will have to be purpose built to fit your space. It is in effect, simply a giant built-in walk-in cupboard that might be used to conceal a compact dressing room, wet room or home office. If music is your thing, you could even have it soundproofed to give you somewhere to listen to your music at full blast or to practise your musical instrument.

Above: *A shiny curving wall creates a dramatic room-within-a-room effect, screening the bathroom from view.*

Opposite: *A floor-to-ceiling cupboard conceals a kitchen. The doors are hinged to slide into the cupboard sides.*

A freestanding room within a room can be as big or as small as you choose – and your space will allow for. It effectively gives you four sides to play with and, if your ceiling is high enough, a top surface, too. If your multi-function space is large enough and your room within a room can be deep enough, you could even try making one side the bathing area, another the kitchen, the third for sleeping and the fourth for sitting. Alternatively, you might make one side a storage wall and, if you have sufficient headroom, put a sleeping platform on the top.

THE ROOM-IN-A-CUPBOARD

The room-in-a-cupboard idea is the simplest configuration of a room within a room. Some kitchen furniture manufacturers now supply mini-kitchens in a cupboard that are ready – bar the addition of the services – to install in your room. Open the doors and there is a tiny sink and hob, oven or microwave, and storage space to boot. Close the doors and the whole thing disappears seamlessly into its surroundings so that you hardly know it's there.

Also available are office-in-a-cupboard arrangements, which provide a neat way of hiding away your work in a multi-function space. Meanwhile, bathroom manufacturers are creating stylish glass-enclosed bathing pods that incorporate a shower and a wash basin. Such a pod would work well on the mezzanine of a multi-function space or in an en-suite bedroom where privacy isn't an issue. If you live in a small studio, you may prefer to choose one with opaque walls of moulded plastic.

If you can't find the room-in-a-cupboard you want, consider having one made to your own specifications. It will be costly, but it could help you maximise the potential of your space.

CASE STUDY

A Room of Boxes

The architect of this loft-type space removed interior walls so that the light from the windows along the two outside walls could be enjoyed to the full. Yet he also wanted to retain separate 'rooms' in the apartment. The solution was to build two box-like rooms within the main space, one housing the kitchen and the other incorporating a guest toilet and washbasin. The rest of the space consists of a living room that is also used for dining and as an office. The bedroom with its en-suite bathroom leading off it adjoins this space.

Working to a strict budget, he grouped plumbing and electricity in one run and used black-veneered chipboard as the main construction material. One extravagance was to clad the kitchen 'box' with sheets of oxidised copper, which has an attractive, red-brown colour.

Despite the dominant black of the chipboard, the 50-square-metre space does not feel cramped. This is thanks to generous natural light, a light-coloured floor in the main living area, white ceilings and the wall of white cupboard fronts.

Above left: *In the kitchen, lengths of chipboard, edges left unfinished, have been used to make shelving and a work surface. Beneath stand a fridge and microwave oven, while a glass panel above helps to separate the kitchen from the living area but without cutting out the light. To the left, doors open to reveal the hob.*

Left: *The two 'boxes' stand on a stone platform. First on the left is the kitchen and to the right is the box that houses the toilet and washbasin.*

Right: *The kitchen 'box', clad in sheets of oxidised copper, benefits from the natural light that pours in from the windows in the wall behind. The panel of glass in the front face of the box gives the kitchen a spacious and open feel.*

Below right: *This part of the space comprises the living area, a dining area and an office. The dining table doubles up as a desk and office paraphernalia disappears behind floor-to-ceiling doors along one wall when not in use.*

Far right: *The wall that separates the bedroom from the adjoining bathroom has clever storage that incorporates bookshelves and wardrobes. Made of the same chipboard as the boxes in the main living area, it forms a decorative link between the two areas.*

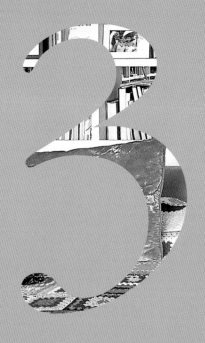

SPACE-
EXPANDING
STORAGE

We've already seen that one of the keys to making your small space work is to cut your clutter and get rid of anything that you can do without. But no matter how many of your possessions you manage to shed, certain things are absolutely essential and you will have to find storage space for them, no matter how small your home.

It is vital that you look at your storage needs right across the board rather than a room at a time. That way you will be better placed to think laterally and spot the potential for storing things in places where you might not expect to keep them. For example, there is no real reason why you should hang your clothes in your bedroom: perhaps they can be stored in a cupboard in a passageway instead. Likewise, you might be able to store books under the stairs rather than trying to fit shelving into the living area.

While you are at this planning stage, you also need to consider what exactly it is that you have to store, what shape and how fragile it is, and how much room it takes up. The type of storage you choose will be determined by such considerations. Clearly, bulky items such as luggage, spare bedding and computer equipment will need a different configuration of storage space from that needed by crockery, glassware, books or DVDs.

There is also the question of how often you use the items. Things that you require on a daily basis obviously need to be close at hand, while those that you use only once or twice a year can go in less accessible places such as at the top of a tall cupboard or on high shelves. Remember, though, that you will still need to be able to reach these places – however occasionally – so you will need to have a ladder, as well as somewhere to store it. One stylish option is a rolling ladder that runs on a track system fitted to the storage unit itself. These ladders are available in a variety of finishes to blend with your furniture, but they do take up some floor space.

Finally, don't forget that there is no point having a bespoke cabinet made to store your CDs, or customising the interior of a wardrobe, without taking into account what your storage needs for CDs and clothing are likely to be a couple of years hence.

Opposite: Every bathroom needs storage space, and in the smallest bathrooms, it should be as streamlined as possible to avoid a cluttered feel. Here, a trio of wooden drawers provides somewhere to stow small items. Their unfussy appearance suits the small space and the wood finish links with the counter top and the bath surround.

Built-In Storage

In a small space, it really does pay to choose built-in storage wherever possible. Freestanding pieces of storage furniture – such as armoires, desks, chests of drawers, bookcases and sideboards – may, if they are designer or antique pieces, look stunning or be unique one-offs, but in a small space they create visual clutter and can make a space look claustrophobic. What is more, there is inevitably a lot of wasted space around a freestanding piece of furniture, whereas built-in storage not only has a more streamlined look, which works best in a small space, but also uses every available centimetre. How else, other than by having built-in, could you achieve storage stretching from wall to wall and from floor to ceiling, or an office in a wall unit that exactly suits your specific requirements?

The principal disadvantage with built-in furniture is that you usually cannot take it with you when you move home – but then you probably won't want to. Having been designed to suit a particular space, a purpose-built or bought piece is unlikely to fit as well anywhere else. If you know that you will be moving in the foreseeable future, you may find it preferable to buy more flexible and versatile modular storage instead so that you can take it with you when you go. Less visually obtrusive than freestanding furniture, it is something of a compromise between freestanding and built-in.

BUILT-IN FOR ALL BUDGETS

You may be concerned at the thought that built-in furniture is very costly, and it is true that it can be, but it doesn't necessarily have to be custom-made.

Mass-market DIY

If you are working to a strict budget, look first at the many mass-market DIY ranges of built-in furniture. You will find a good-looking selection in a wide variety of finishes and styles, but bear in mind your level of DIY expertise when buying. Are your skills such that you can be confident that doors will hang properly, shelves will be level and that the piece will stand straight even if your floors and walls are less than perfect? If not, consider having a professional install the furniture for you, but bear in mind that this is another cost that you will have to factor in.

Design-it-yourself

If both your DIY and design skills are adequate, you could design and make your own piece for a particular space. Alternatively, if your idea is simple enough but you are not much good at DIY, you might be able to have it made relatively cheaply by a local carpenter or handyman. Try using an inexpensive material such as MDF and paint the piece to match your walls. A lick of paint should help conceal any inadequacies in the workmanship.

Specialist fitted furniture

Specialist fitted furniture suppliers mostly produce ranges for kitchens and bedrooms, though some companies also make fitted offices, dining rooms, home cinema systems and bathrooms. Most do a more-than-adequate job and, even though their ranges are mass-produced, many will tailor designs to fit your space exactly. Depending on the company and price point, you may have to do your own measuring up, but from that moment on, many firms will help you with the planning, and they will arrange the fitting, too, if required.

Opposite: *Here, a mixture of open and closed storage prevents the unit from looking too heavy, as does the variation in the way the books are stored – some upright, some lying down – and the occasional use of a decorative object.*

Bespoke storage

At the top end of the market are the bespoke furniture companies, offering the ultimate design-and-build service for a spatially challenged room. These companies will come to your home to measure up, will plan everything with you, suggesting different finishes, configurations and customisation options, will make the furniture to order, and will then come and install it. Supplied in any finish and material you choose, often handmade and designed to fit your needs and your room exactly, bespoke built-in storage furniture can cater for everything.

If cooking is what you love to do, you could have a kitchen that includes wide, deep drawers for storing pots and pans, eye-level cupboards for glassware and crockery, shallow drawers for cutlery (including drawers with individual recesses to fit each of your kitchen knives), plus open shelving and fully integrated appliances if you want them. You could even have a complete kitchen-in-a-cupboard (see page 67).

If you possess a huge collection of clothes – and enough space and money – you could commission storage that will include everything from shallow shelves to deep drawers and hanging space, or even a walk-in wardrobe. If your passion is collecting, you could have an entire wall covered in shelves and niches of all depths and widths, lit from above to show your collection off to best advantage. And if you need a home office, you could have an entire work station built in, with a surface on which to put the computer and storage for all your office essentials ready to hand. Your bathroom could be lined with concealed built-in storage to stow away spare towels and toiletries, while in your bedroom, the bed could be built into a wall of storage that incorporates headboard, bedside storage and lighting.

Above: *Made-to-measure storage is often the best choice for a kitchen, where many varied items need to be stored and readily accessible. Here, unfussy cupboard fronts contain the built-in oven and conceal all kitchen paraphernalia. They also ensure a streamlined look.*

Many also supply freestanding furniture, lighting and accessories to complement their ranges, for instance bedside tables or chests of drawers, matching mirrors or shelving and TV/DVD player stands.

Though they carry only specific designs in certain finishes, most of these fitted furniture suppliers will offer you some degree of customisation, for instance in your choice of interior fitments, door handles or work surfaces. If your budget is limited, many also sell packages that will give you a complete kitchen or office, though you will be restricted to their selection of individual modules rather than units designed to fit your space exactly.

FITTING ALL SPACES

One of the great advantages of built-in storage for small homes is that it can be designed around every architectural irregularity, from arches and uneven ceilings to recesses and alcoves, and it can be made to fit spaces under windows, stairs and eaves. An arch, for example, can be completely filled with an array of different-sized cupboards, shelves, niches and drawers; alcoves and recesses of any shape or size can be fitted with made-to-measure

shelving, cupboards or drawers. If you are looking for somewhere to store your floor mop and ironing board, a cupboard built into a tall narrow recess below the stairs might be just what you need, while a bay window can have a window seat built into it, with storage beneath for books or larger items. Under the eaves in a roof or attic space (see page 95) is another natural place for built-in storage. What you decide to build in will depend on your storage needs; choose from shelves, cupboards or pull-out units on wheels.

Above: *Built-in storage can accommodate every architectural glitch. These shelves make the most of all the space, right up to the curve of the chimney. There is even a niche housing a small TV.*

CONCEAL AND STORE

Building in storage can also help to conceal elements of your home that you would rather not have on show – things such as pipework, boilers, cisterns, and gas and electricity meters. These bulky, unattractive essentials of modern life add to the visual clutter of a space. By building them in, you can achieve a clean, streamlined look and provide yourself with some extra storage space at the same time.

In a bathroom, for example, build in a toilet cistern to waist-height or slightly higher and you will have a deep shelf on top of which to place toiletries. Or continue right up to ceiling level and incorporate a cupboard for cleaning materials or medicines in the boxed-in area above. If space is very tight, you could even have a boxed-in area below the cistern to use for storing cleaning materials or spare toilet rolls. Similarly, if you are concealing a boiler or the gas or electricity meters, extend the boxing-in from floor to ceiling to provide extra shelving or cupboard space.

If you want to conceal the pipework beneath a basin, build in a cupboard with a shelf inside that fits around the pipework to maximise the use of the space. If you are boxing in around a bath, why not try to section off part of the under-bath space and fit a push-catch door to it so that you have a small cupboard for cleaning materials? Alternatively, if there is enough space, allow for a wide ledge at one end of the bath. As well as providing you with a place for toiletries, this could give you an area beneath to use as a small cupboard. Again, it can be accessed by a neat push-catch door.

Above: *Unfussy, beautifully grained wooden cupboard fronts look good in kitchens and living rooms. If you are very short of space, opt for concertina, sliding or upward-opening doors.*

Opposite: *Wall units that reach to ceiling level make the most of the space and create a streamlined look. These have spotlights set in the base to provide task lighting for the kitchen counters.*

MAXIMISING THE SPACE

When you are planning built-in storage, there are some clever pointers to bear in mind that will help you to maximise the space. For a start, think big and build in from floor to ceiling wherever possible. A small cupboard on the wall, or a few rows of shelving, create the same amount of dead floor space below as a tall cupboard or a floor-to-ceiling shelf unit, so it makes sense to continue the cupboard or shelves up or down the wall as far as you can to give yourself the maximum storage space and to avoid wasting space.

Secondly, remember that cupboards require doors and that normal hinged doors take up valuable space when open. Particularly for cupboards in a narrow corridor, or elsewhere in the home where the floor area is limited, it is worth considering other types of doors with different closing options. When you're making your choice, think about the amount of space they will take up as well as the look they will bring to a room.

You could, for instance, try closing off a cupboard with a curtain or with a roller or roman blind, neither of which require any space when open. Curtains are sometimes used for enclosing the space under a sink or to conceal an alcove used for clothes storage. They tend to look relaxed and feminine, though a heavy canvas or linen curtain will work well if you want something rather more masculine in style. A blind looks more businesslike, so it may make a better choice for concealing a home office or music system.

Bi-fold and concertina doors will take up a half or a third of the space of a standard door, depending on the number of panels or folds they have. Again, they look rather businesslike, so like blinds, they tend to work best to enclose bookshelves, media systems and office equipment.

Then there are doors that hinge upwards rather than outwards. These are found mostly in the better-quality built-in kitchen furniture ranges. Bear in mind that, as the open door projects above the cupboard, this type of door won't be suitable for a cupboard that reaches ceiling height. And, as with a normal side-hinged door, make sure there is sufficient clearance for the door to open without hitting you in the face.

Finally, there are sliding doors, and slatted, roll-up doors (which operate like the lid on an old-fashioned roll-top bureau). Neither of these takes up any extra room and you can find them in materials to suit any number of situations, whether for bathroom or kitchen units, for concealing music systems and books, or for hiding clothes and shoes.

CUSTOMISING BUILT-INS

Customising your built-in storage will help to ensure that it works exactly as it needs to to house all your possessions and that the available space is used to the best effect.

Generally, fittings of the highest quality, and with the greatest scope for customisation, are to be found at the bespoke end of the built-in storage market. However, many of the mass-market manufacturers now also offer a wide range of useful additional fitments, particularly for kitchen and bedroom storage systems.

For your kitchen storage, look for corner cabinets, pull-out wine racks, under-sink storage baskets, worktop-mounted scales, hanging shelves, rail and knife-holder systems, and even moulded drawer inserts complete with kitchen gadgets such as graters, can openers and cheese knives.

Bedroom ranges include pull-out clothes-storage bins, shoe racks, trouser racks, tie and belt racks and

BUILT-INS AND ELECTRICITY

If you want to light shelves for books or to provide interior illumination in a wardrobe, or if a cupboard is to house a sound system, TV or computer, your storage unit will need to be wired for electricity. One of the advantages of built-in storage is that such wiring can be concealed neatly inside, especially if the storage unit reaches from floor to ceiling. All the wiring can be run along the back of the unit and plug sockets can be fitted inside cupboards so that even these are not on view.

Lighting inside built-in cupboards is a must to enable you to see exactly what you have got stored in there. The best types of internal lights come on when you open the door, just like a refrigerator light. You do not have to buy bespoke to have lighting incorporated in your built-in kitchen or bedroom storage: even a number of the mass-market manufacturers offer this as an optional extra. Obviously, it makes sense to try to ensure that you can control any lighting inside the cupboard via a standard wall switch, otherwise you will have to go rummaging inside the unit to switch the light on and off.

Built-ins that conceal all your media systems are a great boon, especially in a small space. Media systems can easily clutter up a room with their various different elements – TV, CD and DVD players, speakers, computer, monitor, keyboard and printer, not to mention all their wires and hand-held controls. (Though, thanks to wireless technology, home computers need no longer have lots of trailing wires and music can be piped wirelessly from your computer to built-in speakers anywhere in the house.) A built-in storage unit offers a sleek, streamlined effect that instantly makes a room less busy and hence more spacious.

Above: *This room's retro styling is complemented by a series of quirky cupboards for storing clothing and domestic paperwork and a curtained alcove concealing the music system, TV and DVD player.*

Opposite: *Floor-to-ceiling cupboards provide ample storage space in this small dining room. The seventies feel of the room is enhanced by the moulding on the cupboard doors. Use flush doors for a contemporary look.*

hanging rails, as well as drawer and cupboard dividers.

For customised built-ins for other areas in your home, and for the latest in space-saving fitments, you will probably need to turn to specialist built-in furniture manufacturers and to those who offer a bespoke service. Options include space-saving roll-out corner units, slide-out work surfaces and ironing boards, as well as roll-out kickplate drawers, V-shaped corner drawers and cabinets with dishwasher-style plate storage.

When faced with such a bewildering array of tempting choices, even within the mass-market ranges, it is difficult to know where to start. The key is to keep reminding yourself of exactly what it is you want to store so that you're not seduced by gimmicks and gadgets that you neither really need nor have space for. There is no point having a good-looking pull-out wine rack if you only enjoy soft drinks, or a laundry bin that fits into the wardrobe if you prefer to stow your dirty laundry in a bin near the washing machine.

MAKE IT WORK FOR YOU

Built-in Storage

This amazing six-by-three-metre room provides all that's needed for living, sleeping and cooking, though admittedly on a very small scale. The clever solution to fitting it all in was to line the walls of the room from floor to ceiling with built-in cupboards, drawers and shelving. These gobble up a minimum of floor area while providing maximum storage facilities. The discreet, white-painted finish and invisible touch latches ensure that the visual impact of all those cupboards and drawers is minimised, which helps maintain a sense of space even when there isn't much.

Clever lighting enhances the feeling of spaciousness, especially the concealed lighting above the display shelf, which gives a sense of depth to the room and makes the storage wall above and below appear to 'float', thus ensuring that it doesn't look too dominant. Bench seating built out from the wall completes the picture. Doubling as a bed at night time, it incorporates two full-size mattresses. Bedding is stored beneath the bench seat when not in use.

Opposite: *In a tiny room that has it all, full-height white cupboards form a space-enhancing backdrop that is clean and uncluttered as well as full of hidden surprises. But the room is far from bland and clinical: bold blocks of red in the form of the sofas-beds provide welcoming accents.*

  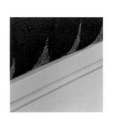  

Eye-level storage
Super-discreet cupboards provide valuable storage in a room that is very spatially challenged. Cupboards that reach the ceiling will give you extra storage space. Match them to the walls for best effect.

Cupboard fronts
The cupboard doors are made of completely plain, white-painted wood and incorporate touch latches to ensure that no handles mar the flush fronts. These space-defying doors are easy to copy.

Floor-level storage
Large, hardly-there drawers beneath the bench seating are fitted with touch latches and provide extra storage for bedding. If possible, fit low-level drawers like these with castors to ensure easy access.

Display shelf
The shelf above the sofa breaks up the expanse of cupboards and provides an attractive display space. Recessed spotlights fitted on the cupboard bases illuminate the collection of objects.

Kitchen-in-a-cupboard
The stainless-steel mini-kitchen, complete with sink, induction hob and fridge, plus storage space for crockery and utensils, can be shut away behind cupboard doors when not in use.

Shelving

Small spaces and open shelving do not always work well together. Unless you consider the location and look of the shelving very carefully and keep the objects that are on view well ordered, you can easily end up with visual clutter that will make your small space feel busy and closed in. And no matter what the size of your living space, items stored on open shelves will inevitably become dirtier and more scruffy than those that sit neatly behind closed doors.

Nevertheless, shelving is an inevitable part of a good storage system. It is the first thing that comes to mind when you have books to store; it will happily accommodate all your CDs and DVDs; and it is likely to be your first choice of place to display decorative items such as vases and bowls, pictures and photographs. In other words, it is extremely versatile.

One of the essentials for living comfortably in a small space is that there should be a good flow of movement around the space. Open shelves play their part in this: you can access items stored on them easily without worrying about which way a cupboard door will open, or whether there is room for it to do so.

Shelving is also generally a cheaper way of storing things than other, built-in storage options. The shelves themselves need not be costly, and as you will probably be able to attach an off-the-peg shelf unit to a wall yourself – even if you have limited DIY skills – you won't face the expense of having to pay a professional to install it for you as might be necessary with built-in cupboard units.

For certain situations, however, it's worth thinking about made-to-measure shelving, which can be designed to fit the tiniest of spaces. Tall narrow gaps that are no use for anything else can be fitted out with decorative narrow shelves to hold a collection of small objects; glass shelves can be installed across a non-opening window, where they will make the most of the light and can be used for display or storage; a shelf unit can be designed to fit a corner anywhere in the home; shallow shelves can be fitted between a kitchen counter and the wall units above to provide a place to store condiments or even to stand a mini sound system to entertain you while you cook. If space is severely restricted, try a fold-down shelf for occasional use, for example as a bedside table in a tiny room.

CHOOSING SHELVING

Wherever possible, choose an adjustable shelving system because this is more versatile: as the collection of things that you want to store grows, you will have the option of changing the shelving configuration to suit.

If you live in a very small space, you might want to choose a material that can be finished to match your walls. This will help the shelves – if not their contents – to 'disappear', which will open up the space visually. Glass shelves achieve the same effect, though, of course, they may not be suitable for holding very heavy items. Very narrow shelving, such as that made from pressed metal, also tends to disappear.

Don't forget to consider the shelf supports, too. Cheap L-shaped shelf supports can be ugly and obtrusive. If the shelves are going to fit in an alcove, look for adjustable shelf supports that fit in the side walls of the

Opposite: *Here, shelving – white, to match the rest of the décor – has been used to divide a living room from the bedroom. The unit is open on both sides, which allows light to pass through and provides a view from one room to the other, enhancing the sense of space.*

SHELVING TRICKS FOR SMALL SPACES

- Try just low-level shelving, at waist-height or a little higher. This works especially well in a low-ceilinged room.

- Shelving at about skirting-board height is even less obtrusive and uses up what would otherwise be wasted space. It makes a good place to store items such as little-used books or CDs.

- Make your shelving do double duty as a room divider, either freestanding or abutting a wall at one end. Even when heavily stacked with books, the shelving will have a lighter feel than would a wall, and the division between the two spaces will still feel quite open and informal.

- Use a mix of shelves and cupboards to make the latter look less dominant and the room feel less cluttered and overpowering.

- Light your shelving. As well as enabling you to see shelf contents clearly, lighting will maximise the open, spacious effect and add a decorative element.

- Keep the contents of your shelves tidy.

- Try to have a unifying theme running through the things you display on your shelves – either a properly thought-out colour theme or a unified collection of objects. Consider putting mismatched items in a row of matching storage boxes or covering books with the same dust jackets to tone with the wall.

Above: *The shelving on either side of this narrow staircase appears to grow from it, helping to anchor the many objects on display on them.*

Opposite: *A series of white-painted shelves in front of a window houses a charming collection of glass and white china that still allows the light to flood into the room.*

alcove and can hardly be seen, or opt for self-supporting, floating shelves, whose clean, contemporary lines make them a good choice for a small space.

For shelves on an area of open wall, try to find neat, compact ready-made units in materials that do not dominate. The unit should look as if it had been made for that particular space; in other words, it should suit the area of wall well – a tall narrow unit in a tall narrow space or a rectangular unit in a rectangular space, for example.

Whatever type of material, supports or shelving units you choose, aim for an unfussy, uncluttered look. Otherwise, your small space will feel hemmed in and claustrophobic.

Unusual Storage Solutions

It may be easy to see how a blank wall could be fitted out efficiently with storage units, cupboards or shelves, but there are many other – sometimes less obvious places – around the home that you could usefully put into service for storage, too.

UNDER AND IN THE STAIRS

If you have stairs, whether leading to the upper floor of a house or to a mezzanine level, you can make the space underneath them work as a storage zone. The simplest option is to use the space to stack up a variety of modular storage units. Choose an assortment of different sizes to maximise your use of the space, tucking in small units where necessary to fill any gaps. You'll need to make sure that you can get at the contents of each one without having to dismantle the whole lot, so choose drawer units rather than boxes with lids. The best way to make this type of storage look good in a small space is to use matching units that will create a unified look, but if you are confident of your design sense, you may be able to get away with a bolder arrangement using an assortment of containers.

Alternatively, go for made-to-measure storage. In most cases this will be a neater, as well as a more space-saving option. The simplest built-in solution is to fit an understairs area with a simple cupboard that matches the slope of the stairs. This will give you somewhere to store big items such as spare bedding, sports equipment or the vacuum cleaner.

A more sophisticated option, and one that uses the space even more efficiently, is to insert a stepped cupboard fitted with a stepped door to match. This will provide you with a large amount of useful space that would otherwise go to waste. If you have smaller items to store, try fitting the understairs space with drawers or with units that pull or roll out.

A final, and unusual, possibility – but one that is suitable for storing only small items – is to insert drawers into the space between the stair risers. The front of each drawer and its handle will be facing you as you go up the stairs. An alternative is to design treads so that they lift up to access a small storage box.

IN THE WALL

If you have a traditional stud and plasterboard wall, you can open up sections of it to use as shallow storage niches. Or if you are building the wall from scratch, you can insert the niches as you go along. Wall niches look very decorative, but will provide you with enough space only for small items. This storage solution especially suits shower areas, wet rooms and bathrooms, where the niches will provide you with handy places for stowing your shampoo and shower gel. In a bedroom, you could store your bedtime reading in a niche by the bed, while in a living room, one would make a great place to display a beautiful object.

If your wall construction isn't suitable for inserting niches, consider building a false wall and putting niches in that. The advantage of this is that you can make the niches any depth you like, so that you will be able to store or display much larger items. The disadvantage is that you will lose some floor space.

Opposite: *These mismatched storage containers, stowed away beneath the staircase leading to a mezzanine, work surprisingly well together. If you choose this sort of arrangement, make sure that you can get at the contents of each one: drawers and mini-cupboards work better than boxes with lids.*

Take the idea of a false wall a stage further by using a double-thickness construction to create a freestanding storage unit. Make it big and use it as a room divider. The wall width will give you plenty of storage space, but as the edge of the wall will also be accessible, you could use this too, neatly fitted out with shelves for storage of small items.

UNDER AND AROUND THE BED

Underbed storage is another effective – and usually completely unobtrusive – way of maximising the storage space in a small home. Nowadays, many beds are already fitted with storage drawers underneath. If yours is not, and you have space under the bed, there is no reason why you cannot buy some ready-made drawers (make sure that you measure the available space carefully before you go shopping), or have some made specially for you.

The best drawers will have castors fitted. This makes them especially suitable for storing heavy items and will help ensure that you do not hurt your back when you pull them out. If you are working to a strict budget, look for low-level boxes or mesh or plastic bags that can be stowed discreetly under the bed.

Another solution – though a more costly one because it will need to be made to measure – is to build a bed base into a platform (see page 60) to provide storage space both under and around the bed. Drawers under the bed, accessed from the side or the end, can offer space to store larger items, while around the bed, little cubbyholes can be used as places in which to keep books and other small items. They can be accessed from above via hinged lids. You could even try building a music system and speakers into the bed base if you wish.

Above: *Building shelves within a wall cavity is a clever space-saving storage solution, and here, even a radiator has been hidden in the wall.*

Opposite: *Sturdy mesh baskets or drawers that fit under the bed provide a home for little-worn or out-of-season clothing or bedlinen. Make sure that the drawers glide out easily.*

LANDINGS AND PASSAGEWAYS

Unless you live in a studio flat, your home will almost certainly include some sort of a corridor, hallway or passageway, and if it is on more than one level, you may well have a landing or half-landing, too. Unless any of these areas are large enough to be turned into another living zone, many of us regard them as spaces with no other purpose than to connect two rooms or floors. However, it can pay to think of them as storage opportunities.

If the space is wide enough, you may be able to include some shelves or a cupboard with a sliding door. If access would be obstructed by either of these options, simply use the top part of the wall, above head-height. This will give you somewhere to store little-used items, such as out-of-season clothing, books you are not likely to read for a while, sports equipment or spare linen. Just ensure that you can reach things when required. A smart-looking ladder is all you need. For a passageway, you might consider a rolling library ladder, which will be easier to manoeuvre than a freestanding one.

ABOVE A DOOR, BELOW A WINDOW

Because these areas have a tendency to 'disappear', they can make good, unobtrusive places to stow things, either in cupboards or on shelves. Cupboards will have a more streamlined appearance, will look less messy and will be easier to keep tidy. Bear in mind, though, that the area above a door is not accessible without a ladder so you should use it only for storing items that you do not need to get at very often.

Above: *A simple bracket-mounted shelf provides useful extra storage above a pair of doors in a corridor.*

Opposite, top: *This off-the-peg adjustable storage rail fits neatly beneath the eaves in an attic room and so uses every bit of space.*

Opposite, bottom: *This freestanding storage wall divides an office space from a bedroom and incorporates a bookcase at the same time.*

OTHER UNUSUAL STORAGE PLACES

Under the eaves

● Use a row of low-level boxes or drawer units that fit the space under the slope of the ceiling. Pull-out units on castors make for easier access.

● Insert a built-in piece to make the most of all the available space and to accommodate the very specific things you have to store.

Under seating, behind seating

● Use the space beneath banquette-style seating as a storage area, perhaps building in some drawers.

● Build deep drawers into the back of banquette seating, in the space between the backrest and the wall.

In the floor

● Fit a floorboard with a flush-fitting handle that, when lifted, reveals a storage box beneath. Super-discreet, such cubbyholes could be used to stow a small safe for your valuables.

Behind a kickplate

● Some of the best kitchen manufacturers now offer roll-out kickplate drawers. These are great places to store baking tins and trays, kitchen towels, napkins and such like.

In a fireplace

● Get a professional in to remove a disused fireplace, finish the space to suit your decorating scheme, and you will have somewhere to store books, magazines, the TV or a music system.

CASE STUDY

Storage Supremo

The nuns who once lived in this building would never recognise the way this 30-square-metre room has been transformed, but they might appreciate the simplicity of its conversion.

It is all thanks to the architect, who, wishing to retain the room's good proportions, designed a single box-like structure to house all life's necessities, then stood it along one wall. As well as incorporating a kitchen and raised sleeping area, he concealed clever storage at every opportunity behind flush-fitting doors and pull-down flaps. When these are not in use, an uninterrupted surface looks out onto the room.

The storage includes a niche for the TV and a cupboard with a pull-down flap for the computer. Alongside are more cupboards, for the printer, stereo system and fax machine. There is also storage for clothes and a even space to put the little stepladder that is needed to reach the bed. And, in the rest of the room, thanks to the box's clever design, there is plenty of space for people to circulate, too.

Below, left to right: *The kitchen consists of a stainless-steel work surface with integrated sink and splashback, and an extractor fan concealed by a red blockboard panel. Heat from the TV and computer escape via small grilles in the front and the niches for each are large enough to leave space for air to circulate. Storage space below the bed houses clothes and the stepladder.*

Above: *A view of the box from the room. A yellow panel screens the bathroom, a door leads to the kitchen, and the upper level contains the bed. In the centre of the box, at just the right height, a niche covered with a Plexiglas screen houses the TV, while the next section along contains the computer. Beneath the bed are tall cupboards for clothes storage.*

Right: *The headboard of the bed, on the mezzanine level, is actually a low, blue-painted wall, which makes a handy place for bedside books and a reading lamp.*

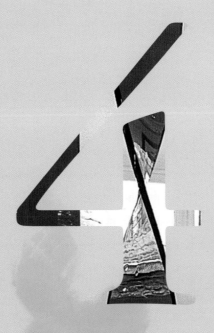

SPACE-DEFYING DECORATING

You can do a lot to give a room a feeling of spaciousness and conceal its small size with a clever use of colour, pattern, texture and lighting – natural and artificial – as well as with reflective and transparent surfaces.

But in general terms, what you need to achieve in the decorative scheme of any room, large or small, is a sense of comfort and of having room to manoeuvre. Realizing such a goal in a small space may seem to be an impossibility, but paradoxically, one way to get there is to think big. Furniture or decorative effects that are slightly over-scaled make a room feel opulent and comfortable: a large sofa, for instance, immediately invites you to sit on it. The received wisdom might be to use a small sofa in a small space, but this will simply underline the room's lack of size, just as filling it with lots of compact pieces of furniture will make a room feel busy.

Obviously, neither should you cram a small room full of large items or cover every surface with brightly coloured and patterned fabrics, wallpaper or decorative objects. Although you should think big, remember that less is more. In order for you to feel comfortable, it is important that you are able to move around the space physically, but also that your eye has somewhere to rest. A long but low sideboard or row of shelving works in a low-ceilinged space because the eye is drawn to the wall above it rather than to the height of the ceiling. Similarly, wall-hung toilets, basins and bidets, which don't conceal the floor, make a small bathroom or cloakroom look more spacious than it really is.

If a lot of storage space is essential, for instance in a small kitchen, you can lessen its impact by providing visual 'breathing space', for instance by fitting a row of eye-level cupboards to the wall with a small gap between each one, by using open shelving above floor units, or by having freestanding units that reveal the floor beneath. These options will all make you feel as though there is space to spare, even though this may be just an illusion.

Opposite: *Many features combine to give this bathroom a feeling of spaciousness. The neutral white and beige colour scheme helps bounce natural light from the skylight around the uncluttered space. Furnishings are simple but beautiful, and the large bath creates a dramatic focal point. The huge wood-framed mirror doubles the space visually and also reflects light.*

Minimalism

Highly influenced by the pared-down aesthetic of traditional Japanese design, minimalism in its purist form reduces everything to the essentials. Emphasis is placed on the structure of the space, and anything that is put in it should enhance that space. This means that neutral colours – usually pure white – prevail, and that sightlines must be kept clear. What little furniture there is – furniture and furnishings are restricted to allow only what is absolutely necessary – is either built-in, low-level or both.

For most people, pure minimalism is difficult to live with. The all-white look can feel cold and clinical and it's very high-maintenance. Let's face it, not many of us are tidy enough to carry off minimalism properly.

Nevertheless, there's no denying that small spaces benefit from simple furnishings and fittings. And the sort of discipline required by minimalism is needed anyway if you are to live comfortably in a small space.

MAKING MINIMALISM WORK

Considering some of these tips from the 'less is more' school of decoration – you don't have to take minimalism to its extremes – will help you to inject breathing space into your small home.

Storage and furniture
Firstly, you need to pare down your possessions, and then get as much as possible of what is left behind closed doors, which means having good built-in storage wherever practical (see pages 74–85). If you can build your furniture in as well, then so much the better, otherwise make sure that your furniture is low level.

Floors and windows
Next, you need to strip down the floors and window frames – literally. Bare floors work best. Depending on your budget, try stone, terrazzo, concrete, ceramic tile, rubber or wood. Leave windows as uncluttered as possible (see pages 116–19).

Colour
Colour for ceilings and walls – including cupboard fronts, unless you decide to make a feature of these – should be restricted to neutrals, preferably white or off-white. You can add interest to the scheme with splashes of colour – strong primary colour works well against a backdrop of white – but make sure that this is well controlled as you don't want the result to look busy.

Texture
Natural materials such as wood and stone look very effective with the minimalist aesthetic and will introduce colour as well as texture. Try using wood for your floor or cupboard fronts, or place a big beautiful sculpture in an eye-catching spot and light it well. Consider stone for counter tops or as a wall surface as well as for floors.

Finishing touches
You can stamp your personality on the room by adding a few accessories, but keep them to a minimum. As with any scheme, you'll need good background and task lighting, as well some lighting to add drama and interest.

Finally, when you have so little in a room, it's important to ensure that everything is of the highest quality. Use the best finishes you can afford and remember that even small details such as door and cupboard handles can take centre stage against a minimal backdrop.

Opposite: What could be simpler than this pared-down minimalist flight of wooden stairs? Fixed to one wall and apparently suspended in space, they do the job they were intended for yet still look light and open. The warmth of the wood prevents them from seeming over-clinical and because of their simplicity, one's eye is drawn to the wood's attractive grain.

MAKE IT WORK FOR YOU

Minimalism

What you need in a small space is a decorating scheme that will enhance the space you have got and provide you with a feeling of leisure and comfort rather than one of cramped awkwardness. Helped by good natural light from a large window on the left, the interior decoration of the living area of this 30-square-metre apartment achieves just that. The architect/owner has kept to a simple colour palette – just white and beige with black and charcoal accents – and low-level furniture that does not block the sightlines. Accessories are pared down, their curvilinear shapes forming a strong contrast to the graphic coffee tables, the dark wood shelf and the tall dark wood freestanding cupboards below. Textural interest is introduced with the rattan chair and its cushion, the low bamboo tables, the linen floor cushions, the chunky wool throws and the space-enhancing, light wood-laminate flooring. Although there is not much furniture, what there is looks comfortable and welcoming, so the effect is far from clinical.

Opposite: *This living room, with its good natural light, simple colour scheme and graphic furniture, is a fine example of how to decorate a small space so it is both aesthetically pleasing and practical. Every element has been chosen with care.*

White walls
White walls help to maximise the sense of space and make a great backdrop for any furniture. If pure bright white seems too cold and clinical, try white with a tint of pink or orange-yellow for more warmth.

Textural interest
With a mainly white and neutral colour scheme, use textural interest to liven things up. Here, the owner has chosen a natural rattan chair that contrasts with a fluffy sheep's wool cushion.

Clear sightlines
Keeping the sightlines clear with low-level furniture – here, piles of linen floor cushions and mobile bamboo plant stands that serve as coffee tables – gives the onlooker some breathing space.

Minimal ornament
A dark wood floating shelf with one or two carefully chosen ornaments creates a focal point without adding clutter that would make the room claustrophobic.

Hidden storage
Keep storage hidden to preserve a sense of spaciousness. To save on cost, this owner has used inexpensive plywood modules with doors made from plasterboard panels that blend with the walls.

Colour

The way you use colour can make all the difference to how large or small your room or home feels. Colour is a very complex subject and to understand it fully you will need to refer to specialised literature and look at useful tools such as a colour wheel, but the few pointers given here will help you grasp the essentials.

UNDERSTANDING COLOUR

Colour can make a space feel larger or smaller. It can also be used to break up an area, to define certain parts of it, or to unify a space. It also adds ambience.

Warm and cool colours
You sense when you walk into a warm cosy room or when a room feels clinical and less inviting. This is because some colours are cool, while others are warm. Colours such as green, blue and purple are described as cool, while red, orange and yellow are warm, but a cool green can be warmed up if you add some yellow to it, while a warm red can be cooled if you add some blue. What is important to know in the context of small spaces, though, is that cool colours look as if they are receding, or moving away from you, while warm ones tend to move towards you. This means that a room with walls painted in a cool blue will look larger than it actually is.

The effect of light on colour
However, things are not always as simple as they appear. The quality of the light plays its part, too, so if you have a room that faces the sun, it will naturally appear warmer than one that faces away from it. This means that a room with plenty of warm, natural light can take a cool colour such as blue, while a room that faces away from the sun could feel chilly with blue walls.

Artificial lighting has an effect on colour, too, and you'll need to take that into account when planning your lighting as well as when thinking about a colour scheme. Ordinary incandescent bulbs are biased towards the red end of the spectrum and so will make the colours in a room look warmer and more yellow than they really are. They will also make blues look more green and reds look more orange. Fluorescent lighting has a mauve-blue bias that makes colours look colder, while halogen lighting gives out a brighter whiter light that is closer to sunlight.

Colour on colour
A colour will also appear to change depending on the colour that is next to it. For example, if you put a pale colour such as mushroom next to another muted colour such as a dull yellow or brown, both colours will look less subdued and more lively.

You also need to know that the larger the area that is covered by a colour, the more that colour will take the lead in a scheme. In a room with white walls and a white floor, the red and green of a painting on the wall will be seen simply as accents.

Tints, shades and harmonies
A tint is made when you add white to a colour, while a shade is obtained by adding black. Lighter colours naturally reflect light, while darker colours absorb it. Harmonies combine tints and shades of colours that are next to each other on the colour wheel, which means, for example, green and yellow, or red and orange. Harmonies are naturally comfortable to the eye.

Above: *The whole of this room could have been painted white, but the chic two-tone wooden moulding strip around the walls helps unify the space, adds depth and personality, and even makes the room feel larger.*

A UNIFIED SCHEME

When you are planning a decorative scheme for an interior, it is important that you consider the area as a whole (that might mean the whole house). In a small space, in particular, you need to choose a colour scheme that will bring a sense of unity to the space. You might, for example, go for a colour scheme based on neutrals or on blues. In the case of a small house, try carrying the chosen colour through every room, varying it slightly from one area to another with changes of tone and shade, picking out different accent colours, perhaps, and adding patterns and textures.

In a small kitchen, freestanding units will give a more spacious look than built-ins because the eye is drawn to the floor under the units rather than stopping dead at the kickplate, but if you prefer the fully integrated look, try and ensure that the units tone with the floor, or at least consider changing the kickplates so that they blend in with the flooring. You might also consider building in your white goods and covering them with panels to match the rest of the units.

Look for materials that match, or are close in colour, or choose finishes that can be painted to co-ordinate with your main colour. If you have an exposed brick wall, for example, this may mean painting it the same colour as the other walls rather than leaving it bare, if the bare brick breaks up the space too much. The texture of the painted brick will add interest that can make up for the loss of colour and pattern of the bare brick.

A unified scheme is also a simple one. So, if you want to highlight a particular feature, use a subtle tint or shade of your main colour, and if you want to add some interest, do so with a considered use of pattern and texture (see pages 114–15). Generally speaking,

if you try to use too many colours or too much pattern, the result is likely to look uncomfortable and bitty and feel cramped and enclosed.

There are, however, exceptions to this rule. A riot of colours and patterns – providing that the former are all tonally similar and the latter are of the same scale – can help blur the boundaries of the space and make it appear larger than it is. Such a scheme can be difficult to get right, however, and is not something for the faint-hearted to try.

Judy 04 © ChasRay 2000 – Copy LV

Above: *The rich wood tones of the sideboard, vases and painting bring these elements together against a white background.*

Opposite: *Pale colours and simple furnishings are not the only way to decorate a small space successfully.*

WHITE AND PALE

It is generally accepted that paler, light-reflecting colours work best in small areas as they have a space-defying effect. The ultimate space-defying colour is, of course, white, but an all-white scheme has its problems, mainly because it is not easy to match white exactly across different materials. It is also very difficult to get a pure white, and this can present a problem if you pick the wrong tint. For example, if you inadvertently use a cool blue-white in a sunless room, the effect will be distinctly chilly. And the reverse is also true – a warm white can make a sunny room feel uncomfortably warm.

In addition, bear in mind that an all-white scheme is high-maintenance. This may not be a problem if you live alone and don't mind cleaning, but it's probably not ideal for a family. Children and/or animals plus white floors or walls is a particularly bad combination!

If you want to benefit from white's space-enhancing properties and don't want to go down the minimalist route (see pages 102–5) – or if an all-white scheme is just too impractical – try limiting white to the ceiling. It can work wonders to open up a small, low-ceilinged room. Or use it just for your cupboard fronts and combine it with the beautiful rich colours and textures of wood and stone elsewhere.

White is not your only option though. Harmonising schemes of any pale cool shades will help to open the space up. Try cool neutrals such as cool off-whites, pale greys, green-greys and lavender greys, or any pale cool green, blue or mauve. Just bear in mind, though, that these colours look best in rooms that have good natural light. If your room lacks this, you will probably need to add some warmth, which you can do subtly with warm greys, beiges and creams, or with apple green or lilac, for instance.

Opposite: *White is the unifying force in this double-height multi-function space. Used for walls, floors, cupboard fronts, bookcases and chairs, it makes the space feel comfortable and generous.*

Above: *White that has been slightly warmed by the addition of pink is used for almost every surface of this tiny twin bedroom. The sense of space is enhanced by the use of sheer voile for the bed hangings.*

USING STRONG COLOUR

Strong colours, as well as textures and bold pattern (see pages 114–15) can be used to add interest to what are, essentially, monochrome schemes. When you add these contrasts, though, it is important not to make the room feel bitty and uncomfortable.

One way to avoid this pitfall is to use contrasting colours that are muted; for example, a dull tone of orange to contrast with cool pale blue, or a soft chartreuse to complement pale lilac. These attractive contemporary combinations will add variety to a scheme without making the contrast feel too harsh and obvious.

Alternatively, you could introduce an accent colour in the form of accessories – a collection of vases or some cushions or throws – or use a beautiful two-tone wallpaper on just one wall, or a fabric panel to make an unusual bedhead.

Boldly contrasting colour can work well too, but limit its use so that it doesn't overpower the space. You could try using a strong colour as an accent, for example a red chair in a pale grey room, or a modern zingy orange roll-top bath in a white bathroom. Alternatively, use it as a focal point, perhaps to paint one wall or a dividing panel, or introduced in the form of a brightly coloured rug.

If you like a vibrant, lively look, you can use larger doses of strong colour. For instance, in a home that consists of several small rooms rather than a large multi-function space, you could paint one of the rooms in a bold colour to make an effective contrast with the rest of the house. The hall is a good place to try this as it's a room that you pass through rather than sit in. If you do want to try such a bold scheme, however, you are advised to keep the other elements of the room – the window and floor treatments and any furniture – as simple as possible.

Left: *In a small house that has been decorated mostly in white and off-white, this lone bedroom makes a bold statement in bright leaf green. The rest of the room has been left simple and uncluttered with only the red chair standing out as a contrast.*

Below left: *This living area in a small apartment has been given a whimsical treatment with red used as an accent colour and touches of bright yellow contrast. Although the colours are bold, the scheme does not feel overwhelming.*

Opposite: *Red can tend to make a space feel smaller, but in this compact kitchen/dining room, its power is offset by plenty of white and some cooling grey.*

Pattern and Texture

A careful – though not necessarily conservative – use of pattern and texture will help to break up a monochrome colour scheme and make a small space look more interesting.

USING PATTERN

Pattern most commonly appears in textiles, flooring and wallpaper, but note, too, the patterns created by window frames, doors and other openings and cupboards. Tall window frames and doors make a room feel taller, but too many of these vertical lines can also have the effect of closing in the walls, which is something to bear in mind if you are tempted to use wallpaper with vertical stripes. The reverse also holds true, so if you want to make a narrow room feel wider, a few broad, contrasting, horizontal stripes painted on the walls will do the trick (see page 107).

Even the grouting used with tiles creates a pattern that can make a small space look even smaller. It is therefore best to use large ones. Additionally, you could lay floor tiles on the diagonal, which will have a 'stretching' effect in a small space.

Contrary to the accepted wisdom that dictates that you should use small

Above: *Strong colour and pattern add a touch of youthfulness to what is essentially a traditional living space. Furniture has been limited so that the small room does not feel cramped despite its lively furnishings.*

patterns in a small room, large patterns in fact work better. Small-scale patterns look too busy and will clutter a small space, whereas bold, over-scaled ones – providing they are used in small doses – challenge the restricted space and add a feeling of liveliness.

To use pattern successfully, you need to break it up so that you experience the breathing space that is essential for a sense of comfort in a room. A brightly patterned pair of chairs will be far less likely to overpower a small room than will a two-seater sofa covered in the same fabric, because of the space between them.

Similarly, if you want use a boldly patterned wallpaper, don't cover an entire room with it, but instead use it on one wall or on a panel or half-wall. You may even get away with using more than one pattern: just ensure that the patterns you choose are of a similar scale and tone.

If you have a collection of favourite objects that you want to display, bear in mind that they also create a pattern, so resist the temptation to put them all on show unless they have a unifying theme, such as their shape or colour. A collection of small disparate items looks fussy and cramped, whereas a unified collection appears as one large element. If in doubt, choose a single over-scaled piece and light it well.

USING TEXTURE

Textures also create patterns in a room in the way that they subtly reflect or absorb the light. They are a great way to add variety and depth without creating fussiness, and they are important as a contrast in white and neutral schemes. A combination of contrasting textures will add further interest: think of a rough sisal mat with a smooth limestone floor, or a shiny metallic sculpture with a shag-pile carpet.

You can add textures to your small-space scheme in the form of different paint finishes, flooring, cabinet fronts, work surfaces, accessories and textiles. Bear in mind that cool neutrals all work especially well with natural textures and materials such as stone, wood, silk and wool. Indeed, textures could be the starting point for your decorating scheme.

Soft textures are essential for comfort in a home – think of thick wool throws, fluffy towels and large squashy cushions. We need the contrast they provide with the many noisy hard surfaces that are an inevitable part of any modern home. Use these soft textures generously, and they will not only make you feel good, but will also help to challenge the smallness of your space.

Above: *In this tiny bathroom, a metal chain curtain creates a screen and adds pattern, as it filters the light, as well as texture to an otherwise simple decorative scheme. The metal chain echoes the shiny brass washbasin and both help to reflect light around the room.*

Above: *Bring the outside in wherever you can. This small living area enjoys great views of the garden and sky thanks to unadorned windows, the large expanse of glass roof and the door that opens straight into the garden.*

Lighting and Windows

Nothing will make your space feel smaller than a lack of light. A room that has shadow-filled corners looks smaller than a light and airy one, and if you have to work without sufficient light, you will feel cramped and uncomfortable. It follows that, in small spaces particularly, you must do all you can to maximise the light you have got and find ways of adding to it where necessary.

Unfortunately, when most of us think about devising a decorating scheme, we hardly give a thought to the presence or lack of natural light in the space. And when we think about the sort of artificial lighting we're going to install, we often make our choices based on the look of a particular fitting rather than on the usefulness of the light it produces for a given purpose.

Interior designers tell us, though, that lighting should form an integral part of our planning, whatever the size of the space. They advise us to think of lighting in terms of a series of layers that are built up, one on top of the other. The first, and probably the most important, of these is the natural light to be gained from windows and other openings.

NATURAL LIGHT

Natural light enters your home through windows, so what better way to improve on what you have got than by increasing the size of existing windows or adding some new ones? If you are able to do so, this will not only bring more light into a room, but will also help to connect you with the outside world, which, in turn, will make your space feel bigger. If you can look out over a garden, roof terrace or even a cityscape as you sit working in your tiny office, the walls of the room will tend to disappear as you become part of the view outside. (For more on how you can change what you've got by adding windows, see pages 34–5.) Bear in mind, though, that lots of glass can make a room hot, so large windows or a conservatory will benefit from being fitted with special solar-control glass rather than with standard glass.

Another way of bringing more natural light into your space is to remove internal walls and doors and either leave openings, use half-height or half-width walls, or fill the opening with glass. All these options will enable light to pass from one area to another, will open up views – of other areas in the house or of the outdoors – and will provide you with a greater sense of space. (See also pages 32–6.)

Below: *This dark-toned bedroom breaks the rules about using a pale palette of colours in small spaces. But plenty of natural light pours into the room through the huge floor-to-ceiling French window, which opens onto a balcony with views beyond. Light is also reflected by the bold mirror situated above the bed.*

WINDOW TREATMENTS

Having got as much light flowing into your home as you can, it makes sense not to impede it with fancy blinds and curtains. What is more, these tend to look fussy and will have the effect of closing the room in. It is far better to leave windows bare if at all possible, or, failing that, to stick to the simplest of window treatments.

If bare windows are not an option because you are overlooked, or because you need screening from early morning sunlight, opt for simple blinds such as slatted wooden or metal ones, vertical types, or roller or roman blinds. Alternatively, choose fine sheer curtains or linked sliding panels that are pulled by a draw rod and that slide behind one another.

Just make sure that, when open, whatever window treatment you choose is well out of the way of the window. This may mean setting blinds well beyond or above the window frame.

With curtains, provided you have adequate wall space on either side of the window, fit a track or pole that extends beyond the opening so that the curtains or curtain panels will pull back to clear it.

If privacy, but not the intrusion of sunlight, is an issue, another solution is to use decorative or frosted glass in a window instead of clear glass. It may be that you need obscure only part of the glass (normally the lower part), to give you the privacy you need. Windows can be professionally fitted with obscured glass, but if you are on a very tight budget, you could try a DIY solution such as an adhesive window film or spray-on frosting. At the other end of the cost spectrum, another option is a type of high-tech glass that changes from clear to opaque at the flick of a switch.

If you want a treatment that will soften the window without blocking the light, try using a simple valance on a pole over the window.

Above left: *Simple internal shutters effectively shut out the light in this bedroom. The fine linen curtains that run from wall to wall make the room seem larger.*

Above right: *This tall, dramatic pair of windows has been left unadorned to maximise the light, save for a softening valance of voile above each.*

Opposite: *Simple window treatments always work best in small spaces. An all-white colour scheme further enhances the sense of space.*

Above: *In this living/dining area, powerful wall lights direct a strong beam onto the white ceiling to* *envelop it in light. Accent lighting in the form of table and floor lamps spotlight a couple of decorative objects.*

ARTIFICIAL LIGHT

In a small space, you need lots of light, and to ensure that it is as flexible as possible, you should have plenty of sockets, switches and dimmer controls.

Your lighting must also be as space-saving as possible, so the best choices are lights that can be installed in ceilings, under wall units, on walls and in the floor. Floor-standing lamps and table lamps take up valuable space, and too many of them can make the room look busy. In a bedroom, try bed- or wall-mounted reading lamps or various types of clip-on lamps.

The quality of the light you get from different light sources will also affect the sense of space in your room. Everyday tungsten light bulbs give out a warm, yellowish glow that can be used to make a space feel cosy. Halogen lighting, on the other hand, emits a very crisp white light that adds sparkle and will help to open up a small space.

LIGHTING LAYERS

Any successful interior will have a mixture of different types of lighting, which should be built up in layers according to their purpose.

Ambient lighting
Nothing is worse than using a solitary ceiling light to provide your ambient lighting: it leaves the corners of the room bathed in gloom. A better solution is to install lots of recessed downlights in the ceiling – they will make a low-ceilinged room look larger – or to use track lighting. For ambient light over a dining table, another option is to have a versatile pendant light with a rise-and-fall mechanism. If you really must have a centre light, make sure that there are plenty of other light sources in the room as well, including wall lights, uplighters and downlights, to add variety.

Directional lighting
Concentrated directional task lighting will be needed for working or reading. This can take the form of downlights fitted beneath a wall cabinet in the kitchen or beneath shelving in an office, or it may be provided by a simple adjustable desk lamp or floor reading lamp. If you are using under-cabinet lighting, make sure that it is fixed near the front of the cabinet or you will find yourself working in your own shadow.

Accent lighting
Accent, or decorative, lighting can be provided by spotlights, striplights or wall washers. Used for illuminating things such as paintings, houseplants, bookshelves and architectural details – as well as sometimes for purely decorative effect – this type of lighting adds a sense of drama and theatricality and is a very useful tool for enhancing the sense of space. When you illuminate one feature so that it stands centre stage, the walls around tend to dissolve, making the whole space feel larger.

Above: *A curved backlit white Plexiglas panel between the floor and wall units in this tiny kitchen gives the feeling that the edges of the room go on to infinity. The concealed lighting adds extra ambient light, supplementing recessed spotlights in the ceiling.*

- Make the walls of a small room 'dissolve' away by dimming the ambient light and cloaking the walls in darkness.

- Paradoxically, you can also make walls dissolve by bathing them in light. Use wall washers on a light-coloured ceiling and walls, or try discreet-looking uplighters to bounce the light where you need it.

- Make sure that all corners of the room are well lit. Try using uplighters, lights set into the floor or table lamps.

- To make a ceiling feel higher, use a row of uplighters hidden behind seating along one wall.

- Another way of making a ceiling feel higher is to use low-slung pendant lights. These cast a strong concentrated pool of light downwards so the area above dissolves and you do not notice the lack of height.

- Creating a sense of movement through the space via lighting can help make a room feel larger. Try a row of spotlights along a corridor floor or ceiling to lead the eye away from the narrowness of the corridor and on into the next space.

- Creating a panel of light at one end of a space, for instance by backlighting a bookcase on a wall, will lead the eye beyond the immediate surroundings.

- Hidden lighting can make a space feel larger. Try hidden uplighters, or backlight a wall of shelving. The wall behind dissolves so that you lose the sense of where it really is.

- Backlight a bathroom mirror or cabinet and there will appear to be space behind it.

- Use strip lighting above and below a row of eye-level wall cabinets, above and below a floor-to-ceiling cabinet, below a bed or round the edges of a false ceiling. The cabinets and the bed will seem far less bulky and the ceiling will appear to 'float'.

- Try lighting concealed behind translucent panels. It sheds an attractive diffused light and makes it difficult for the eye to perceive the depth of a space. Try it in a small kitchen, in the space between the work surface and the wall cabinets, or simply use cabinets with translucent panels in the doors, and install lighting inside.

- Set lights flush in the treads of the stairs leading to a mezzanine or in the wall flanking the stairs. These will not only serve the practical purpose of indicating where the stairs are, but will also help direct the eye from zone to zone.

Above: *A row of industrial-style pendant lights above the work surface in this low-ceilinged mini-kitchen casts concentrated beams of light that disguise the lack of height in the room.*

MAKE IT WORK FOR YOU

Lighting and Windows

In the tiny no-frills kitchen of this loft apartment, ensuring maximum light was a principal aim. This has been achieved by leaving the huge countertop-to-ceiling window uncluttered by any blind or other window treatment so that the view to the courtyard below remains unobstructed. Even the shelving in front of the window is made of glass to allow as much light in as possible. And, in order that the light be allowed to permeate other parts of the apartment too, the dividing walls between the kitchen and the living area and between the kitchen and the bedroom are also translucent. The light-enhancing effect of the large window is boosted further by the white walls and appliances, and metal has been used elsewhere in the room to help bounce the light around the space. The lightness of the space softens the somewhat brutalist and industrial style of the kitchen (evidenced notably in the exposed ventilation pipe and the use of concrete for the work surface), as do small splashes of colour introduced in the form of accessories.

Opposite: This tiny kitchen is saved from being claustrophobic by the generous use of glass, reflective surfaces and white walls. Structural elements such as the window and door frames are left simple and graphic to help retain the uncluttered look.

Large window
A huge, curtainless, picture window ensures that the natural light – and the view – can be enjoyed to the full.

Mirrored glass wall
The graphic grid pattern of the window frame is echoed in the metal framing of the mirrored glass wall, which provides a some privacy for the adjacent bedroom.

Glass shelving
In a room with limited wall space, shelves set in front of the window are a boon. These shelves are made of glass, supported on metal brackets, so any loss of light is reduced to a minimum.

Light-reflecting metal
The ventilation pipe clad in metal and the zinc-covered floor and doors of the kitchen base units help to bounce the natural light around the space.

White walls
Painting the walls white and having white kitchen appliances helps to unify the decorating scheme and increases the feeling of spaciousness in this tiny kitchen.

Reflection and Transparency

Using reflective surfaces such as mirror and metal in your decorating scheme will bounce the light around and help give a sense of spaciousness. And if you also use see-through surfaces – glass and Perspex, for example – the light in your room can flow through unimpeded. A space filled with metal, mirror and/or glass would not only be totally impractical, but would also produce a very strange, cold and challenging environment – not the sort of place where most of us would want to live. Nevertheless, if you use these materials judiciously, you will see the difference they can make.

WALLS AND CEILINGS

Walls and ceilings constitute the largest overall surface area of a home and so have the biggest impact. They offer plenty of opportunity to introduce materials with a reflective quality or some transparency.

High-gloss paint

High-gloss paints, lacquers and varnishes will all give a really hard, tough gloss, and one wall painted in glossy lacquered colour or a metallic-effect paint will look dramatic, especially in a small space. If an ultra-shiny finish doesn't appeal, then try paint with just a slight sheen or one with a glitter-effect or opalescent finish. Used on the ceiling, especially in conjunction with good lighting (see pages 120–22), this can be particularly space-enhancing.

Wallpaper

Wallpaper has recently made a fashion comeback and those with light-reflecting metallic finishes are a great way of injecting a decorative element as well as a reflective surface into a small space. Because they have a strong visual presence, they look best used as a focal point on a single wall or as a panel.

Mirror surfaces

Mirror is the most obvious choice for a light-reflecting wall surface, but it must be kept spotless for it to look good. A great location for a large expanse of mirror is the bathroom – providing you do not mind seeing yourself naked. It adds a feeling of freshness and vitality, and if you cover opposite walls of a small windowless bathroom with mirrors, the room will immediately feel less closed in.

Use mirror with good lighting for best effect, and if you can, locate an expanse of mirror opposite a window or door. You could also try using mirror in conjunction with decorative lighting behind a bookshelf or behind a shelf that holds a display of your favourite objects. Positioning a mirror between

Below left: An unusual feature of this small bedroom is the copper-coloured, highly reflective suspended ceiling over the bed. As if by magic, the room feels almost twice the size. To achieve a similar effect more cheaply, try high-gloss lacquer or metallic wallpaper instead. Either would work well on a wall too.

Opposite: Orange and brown suggest warmth and enclosure and so tend to make a space feel smaller. In this tiny retro-style bathroom, however, their effect has been mitigated by an entire wall of mirror that helps to bounce light around the space.

two windows is another useful ploy, while simply standing a large mirror on the floor propped against a wall looks contemporary and you may be able to place it opposite a window to provide additional light reflection.

Your choice is not restricted to framed mirrors or to large mirrored panels. An alternative is mirror tiles, though it is best to avoid small ones as the joins will create a busy look that doesn't suit small rooms. Nor are you limited to plain mirror. Tinted mirror in pale blue, green or grey may suit your decorative scheme, though it will not be quite so good for practical purposes, such as shaving or applying makeup, of course.

Tiles

Although they are less light-reflecting than mirror, tiles – glazed ceramic, metal or glass – are another option for your walls. Glazed ceramic tiles are hard-wearing, available in a wide range of formats and colours – white or fairly neutral ones often work best in a small space – and are versatile enough to work in any scheme. There are also some good-looking contemporary designs that will add a decorative element to a kitchen or bathroom.

Metal tiles in stainless steel and copper come with a satin or textured finish and can be used on walls, for instance as a splashback, as well as on counter tops. Glass tiles look slightly 'watery', which makes them especially effective in a bathroom. They, too, are available in a wide range of attractive colours and formats.

Glass

Glass walls really enhance a sense of space. As well as clear glass, you will also find sandblasted, etched, textured and screen-printed glass – the latter offering interesting design and colour opportunities – and even a high-tech glass that changes from clear to

opaque at the touch of a button. Glass bricks offer another decorative effect: they are great for walls and they, too, come in a range of colours.

Since safety is an issue with sheet glass, you will need to use structural-quality glass that is shatterproof. In addition, glass wall panels may need to incorporate an element of pattern – a sandblasted design, perhaps – to advertise their presence, otherwise you and your guests may find yourselves walking into them. It goes without saying that glass should be installed by a professional.

Above: *Transparent and reflective materials have been used on virtually every surface in this bathroom.*

Opposite: *In this bedroom under the eaves, glass bricks enclose an en-suite bathroom to allow light from the bedroom to flow through unimpeded.*

FLOORS

A shiny floor is not necessarily slippery (though some surfaces are when wet), so there is no reason why you cannot have a glossy floor finish if you wish. Try high-gloss paint, which comes in a range of colours, use gloss varnish over paint or wood, or opt for a floor laid in high-gloss wood laminate. Alternatively, consider the following:

Ceramic tiles and stone
One mid-sheen option is to use floor-quality glazed ceramic tiles, though make sure you choose non-slip finishes in areas that get wet, such as kitchens and bathrooms. A more costly alternative is stone, which you can also use on walls. For maximum light-reflecting qualities, go for a highly polished finish, which is most commonly found in granite, though this is slippery when wet. An advantage of stone is that it comes in a huge range of types and colours; a drawback is its weight. Check that your floor joists are able to support the weight; if not, you will need to have them strengthened.

Metal flooring
If you like a high-tech or industrial look, light-reflecting plate metal or open-grid metal flooring or stairs may be worth considering. Metal floors are extremely tough and are available with non-slip surfaces and in a variety of styles, materials and colours. They are also easy to keep clean.

Polished concrete
Concrete has progressed from being a utility material to a luxury one, with the result that polished concrete flooring is now often found in architect-designed homes, galleries, shops and restaurants. As well as offering a highly reflective surface that suits a small space, it will give a cutting-edge industrial chic look. It can be coloured if you wish and

Right: *Transparent and reflective surfaces abound in this stylish kitchen. The high-gloss floor, metallic cupboard fronts and shiny lacquered red wall panel help reflect the light, while the sandblasted glass panel set in the red wall and the red glass table both add a sense of light and transparency.*

poured, or laid in tiles or made-to-measure panels, but all require a suitable sub-base. It can be laid as thin as 5mm, so there is no problem if you want to use it in an upstairs room. It is extremely durable and easy to maintain.

Resin

Poured and polished resin is durable, low-maintenance and offers an industrial chic look in any colour you fancy. Its highly glossy surface will really bounce light and colour round a room.

Glass

Glass is a cutting-edge option for stair treads or floor panels but bear in mind safety considerations (see page 129): for use underfoot, it needs to be non-slip as well as shatterproof.

FITTINGS AND FURNISHINGS

Fittings and furnishings in light-reflecting or transparent materials can also be used to enhance the sense of space. If you have a large expanse of built-in storage, consider breaking it up with mirrored cupboard fronts, which are especially useful in a bedroom or dressing area. Or you could try translucent panels in the doors and drawers for a similar effect. If you want to incorporate a lot of cupboards in a small room without overwhelming the space, for example in a kitchen, fit those at eye-level with translucent-panel doors instead of with solid doors. And for even better space-enhancing results, backlight them.

Another light-reflecting option – and one that will put you firmly at the cutting edge of interior design – is to use stainless steel for kitchen cupboard fronts and appliances. Stainless steel is a tough surface, but bear in mind that it needs to be kept free of fingermarks if it is to look good, and that is not always easy to achieve in the kitchen.

You can introduce shiny metal in other ways, too. Of course, taps in chrome, brass or even gold-plate will introduce some sparkle to the kitchen or bathroom, but you could also consider a metal basin or bath.

Mirrored furniture is available in a wide variety of styles of chests of drawers, dressing tables, console tables, desks and cupboards. It is very fashionable, though not cheap, and, as with most reflective surfaces, needs to be kept clean for it to look its best.

Finally, look out for fabrics that include light-reflecting metallic thread, such as self-effacing voile, which makes a good choice for lightweight curtains. Bolder, heavier-weight fabrics, such as shiny satins, lamé or fabrics with metal-thread embroidery or metallic ribbon trim, can be used for throws, bed coverings or as cushion covers.

Opposite*: Sleek, stainless-steel units reflect the light in this tiny kitchen and help to make it feel bigger. The fact that you can see the floor beneath them also enhances the space, as does the light-coloured floor. The black-tiled splashback makes a strong contrast and helps define the kitchen area.*

Left: *Even a small piece of shiny furniture can make a difference to the sense of space in a room. If you want to achieve a similar effect but with a more feminine look, try a mirror-fronted chest of drawers or cabinet.*

Opposite: *Light floods in from a large window and is bounced around the room by the crystal droplets of an antique chandelier. The light-coloured palette and the white blooms in a clear glass vase all help to enhance the sense of space.*

Right: *Perspex is available in a wide range of colours, textures, sizes and thicknesses. Here, twisted strips of coloured Perspex create a dazzling curtain effect.*

TRANSPARENT MATERIALS

In addition to being used for windows, dividing panels or walls and flooring, glass has other applications in the home, and there are other transparent materials to consider, too.

Glass

Glass also plays its part in the traditional chandelier or in its modern counterpart, which is often composed of a mixture of glass droplets and shiny chrome. When the lights are on – or the candles are lit – the glass droplets enhance and magnify the light and will add sparkle to any small room.

Nor should you forget glass furniture. You will find some eye-catching tables and nests of tables that are practical additions to a room as well as being decorative and space-enhancing.

Glass is also a good choice for shelving, and looks great when lit from underneath. Used for shelves in front of a window, it will give you useful display space without limiting the light.

Perspex

Almost as good as glass for its light-reflecting qualities, Perspex is used for a wide range of small furniture, including chairs, console tables, coffee tables and smaller nests of tables. It wins hands down on safety grounds and is strong and scratch-resistant, and you only need to wash it with soapy water to keep it looking good. It also comes in a variety of tints, though of course these will not reflect the light as effectively as the clear version.

Transparent fabric

Finally, do not forget the possibilities of transparent fabrics such as voile or muslin. As well as being popular materials for shading windows, they make a great choice for curtains around a bed or to screen off part of a room without blocking the flow of light.

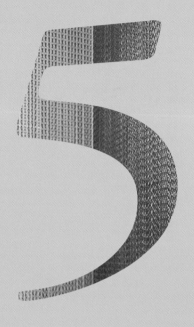

SPACE-SAVING
FURNISHING

Now that you have made the most of your small space in terms of structure, storage and decoration, the time has come to consider how to add in all the furniture that you need to make your space liveable. Although a small space may set severe limits on what you can physically fit in, don't be daunted: there are ways to reduce the scale and impact of your furniture without compromising on comfort.

You may not want to go down the minimalist route of furnishing (see pages 102–5), but you do need to minimise the visual impact of any furniture that you have. The first thing you can do to achieve this is to keep the floor area as clear as possible, and that means ensuring that as much of your furniture as possible is built-in, as freestanding furniture takes up a lot of floor space. In addition to storage (see pages 74–85), consider whether you could build other elements into your space – built-in seating, beds or a desk, for example. Some of these options can be designed to serve two purposes and so save even more space (see pages 148–53).

Built-in seating is generally bench seating, which is commonly reserved for use in kitchens, but there is no reason why you cannot build a low platform in a living room, top it off with comfortable cushions and provide further cushions as a back rest. Make it part of a storage wall configuration and add space for storage beneath the platform, and you have a very functional, unobtrusive solution that will answer several needs in one go.

Built-in beds can save a huge amount of space if they are of the foldaway variety, and a number of these also incorporate a desk and/or storage. If a foldaway bed is not an option, consider building one on a platform and using the space beneath for storage, or at least try to back your bed with a storage unit that doubles as a headboard and bedside table. A built-in desk can also save you space, especially if you need to use it only occasionally. If necessary, it can consist of nothing more than a shelf fixed between two storage units, or a pull-out shelf built into one (see opposite), on which you could perch a laptop.

Opposite: Here, the back wall of a mezzanine has been fitted with a row of bespoke walnut cupboards that conceal a TV and wardrobes. Most ingenious, though, is the way a shelf pulls out and a cupboard door opens to provide the neatest of little office areas. When the chair is not in use here, it makes a useful bedroom chair.

Compress, Fold, Stack and Pull

There are certain items that you simply cannot do without, even in a spatially challenged home. If you can't build them in, one obvious way to get round the problem of fitting it all in is to look for furniture that is particularly small – though you must be sure that it is able to do its job adequately. Alternatively, look for pieces that can be folded away or stacked when not in use, or can be pulled-out or extended when needed.

COMPACT FURNISHINGS

Filling a tiny space with small furniture can make it look bitty and smaller still, so use compact furniture judiciously. Of course, it needs to be comfortable, too. You might want to look out for a small table – just big enough for a snack or for perching a laptop on – and some are wall-hung to take up even less space, but where compact furniture really comes into its own is in the kitchen and bathroom, and there are lots of options to choose from.

Kitchens

Kitchen appliance manufacturers now supply a wide range of slimline or compact fridges and dishwashers, ovens and compact microwave ovens. Obviously they won't hold as much as a full-size version, but if you live on your own, or with just one other, they may well be big enough for you. You can even find compact range-style ovens if that is the look you are after.

You might be able to do away with a standard oven altogether and opt instead for a combination microwave/oven/grill. These are larger than a regular microwave oven, but can be built in to save space. They do not offer the flexibility that you will get with separate appliances, but if your kitchen space is minuscule, you don't do much cooking, or you are designing a kitchen for a second home where relaxing is more important than cooking, it may be a compromise worth making.

Then there are small, modular hobs with the space for just one or two pans. As in the case of a combination microwave/oven/grill, these are fine in certain situations, but they will challenge you if you need to use them to cook regularly for a family.

If you have a dishwasher, you really need only one sink rather than a pair. A compact sink should be fine if you do not do a lot of cooking or entertaining, but you will struggle to fit a large roasting tin or oven shelf in one. A corner sink takes up half the worktop area of an equivalent rectangular one and models often incorporate a draining board and/or other accessories such as strainers and chopping boards.

Bathrooms

Compact basins and toilets are ideal for a small bathroom or for a guest cloakroom. There is a wide range of models in all materials and you don't have to compromise on looks or

Opposite:
Furniture that hugs the wall saves vital floor space. This space-age style room uses semi-circles as the motif for a made-to-measure, wall-hung light fitting, table, shelf and TV/DVD stand, all in seventies-style laminate.

Below: *Mini-kitchens require mini appliances. Fortunately, many manufacturers now produce compact sinks, fridges, dishwashers, hobs and ovens. If you cannot find the kitchen sink you are looking for, do as the owner of this space did and consider bathroom ranges.*

Above: *This tiny washbasin would fit into the smallest of spaces, yet even incorporates a soap dish and a hook for hanging a towel.*

Opposite: *Here, a tiny dining area has been created out of not much more than an alcove with a window. There is just room for a few chairs and a garden table with a fold-down top. Save even more space by using chairs that either fold or stack.*

usefulness, though the tiniest basins, some not much more than a wall-mounted tap with a tray beneath, may be suitable only for a cloakroom. Look out, too, for corner basins and slim basins that make up for in length what they lack in depth. The latter are especially suitable for building into a narrow counter top.

Consider corner baths, baths that taper and compact models – but check that they are big enough to lie down in. You could even have a smaller version of the traditional roll-top bath. If you don't have room for even a compact full-length bath, try a squat one that incorporates a seat. That way you can take a shower standing in the deep section or enjoy a wash while seated.

Of course, doing away with the bath altogether and installing a shower is the most space-saving solution. Corner showers pods come in square, rectangular or semi-circular shapes and, like corner baths, ensure that no potentially useful floor space is wasted.

STACKING FURNITURE

Furniture that you can stack is another, versatile, way of dealing with the problem of fitting it all in. It will enable you to leave out what you need for everyday use, while keeping spares on hand for when you have guests.

Chairs

There is plenty of choice when it comes to good stacking chairs, many of which were originally designed for commercial use. Following in the footsteps of Arne Jacobson and his Ant chair, modern designers have come up with a wide range of attractive and comfortable chairs made in moulded plastic or veneer and chrome, and they are available at all price points. If you like a fifties look, try chrome stacking chairs or stools with padded leatherette seats.

Beds

Stacking single beds usually have wooden frames and so are quite heavy to separate. More versatile and less unwieldy is the type with a lower bed that glides on castors and has spring-loaded legs that make it easy to raise and lower. You could also consider a single divan on folding legs that operates on a similar principle.

Any of these is fine for occasional use, but bear in mind that you probably would not want to sleep on one all the time, nor have to pull it out on a daily basis. Remember, too, that you will need to find somewhere to store bedding for the second bed.

Tables

Nests of tables are something of a cliché but they are coming back into fashion. Look out for vintage models or contemporary versions in wood, glass, Perspex or acrylic. Perspex and acrylic tables have the advantage of suiting any décor, traditional or modern.

FOLDING FURNITURE

Some foldaway furniture disappears altogether when not in use; other types simply take up less space. This sort of furniture may first have been conceived for use by soldiers on the move, but it has come a long way since then, and there are now designs to suit everyone.

Foldaway beds

A wall bed, which folds away into a cupboard, is very useful for a room that has to do double duty as a bedroom/study or a bedroom/living room. The off-the-peg bed frame, which is raised and lowered effortlessly by a spring-loaded counter-balancing system, is fitted into your own wall furniture. Once the bed is folded away – along with the bedding – you see only a cupboard front, so the effect is very streamlined.

There have been a few stories of people being folded away in these beds, so make sure when you buy that the mechanism meets safety standards.

Also available are bunk beds that fold flat against a wall. Some of these fold away into a neat cupboard, like a wall bed, while others leave just a pair of unobtrusive panels on view. These are very useful for solo living spaces or for children's rooms.

Chairs and stools

Folding chairs and stools are a ubiquitous space-saving solution. The best known version is probably the director's chair in traditional wood and canvas, or the more upmarket version in chrome and leather. Similar in construction to the director's chair, but looking more like an armchair and giving greater back support, is the tripolina chair based on a mid-19th century design for British officers.

Other simple folding chairs come in metal, wood, or a combination of metal and plastic. There are even corrugated cardboard versions that are quite sturdy, though they clearly cannot be expected to last a lifetime. All of these are great for saving space, but only those that have cloth or leather seats could truly be called comfortable. It is probably best to save the others for occasional visitors.

Tables

Options for folding tables include gateleg and drop-leaf types, plus fold-down tables and folding trestles that you can use to support a tabletop. You may also find wall-mounted, fold-down seating and tables, the sturdiest of which incorporate foldaway legs or a supporting strut.

Gateleg and drop-leaf tables have been around for years, but look out for models in contemporary designs, many of which are large enough to seat four people comfortably. Many fold-down tables look disappointingly utilitarian, but there are also some good-looking folding trestle legs, which you can top with the surface of your choice, be that glass, wood or MDF. These work well for dining and make good work surfaces for a home office, too.

PULL-OUT AND EXTENDING FURNITURE

Furniture that can be pulled out from another piece of furniture (or that pops up from one) to provide an extra surface or function is another useful option for the space-poor home, as is furniture that can be extended when needed.

Pull-out furniture

The most basic pull-outs are shelves and counters: the very simple extra work surface that can be pulled out from a kitchen base unit, for example, or the shelf that you can pull out from a piece of made-to-measure, built-in furniture to give you a desk. Make sure that any such shelf is sturdy enough to support the weight of whatever you need to put on it. A slightly more sophisticated option is the ironing board that stows away neatly away in a base unit when not in use.

If cost is not an issue, the options are endless: you might consider building a pop-up table into a specially constructed floor, having a pull-out table and seating that slots into a wall unit, or installing an electrically controlled TV screen that pops up from a base unit, for example.

Extending tables

A much more common and affordable choice, extending tables have been around for a long time and there are now many versions on the market. Most consist of a table in two sections that pull apart to reveal an extending leaf or leaves hidden within. Some of

Left: *This multi-purpose room incorporates many space-saving devices, but one of the most eye-catching is the rosewood cabinet. For a start, it forms an elegant low-level divide, enabling someone to be in the kitchen without feeling cut off from the living area. Its top surface provides a resting place for ornaments or for food being passed between the 'rooms'.*

the more modern designs are in a single piece that sits on an extending frame that pulls out to reveal the leaf or leaves. (Simply lift the leaf out, slot it between the main section of the table and frame, then push the frame closed.) Extending tables are very useful if you like entertaining as a number can extend to seat as many as ten or twelve people, but make sure your room can accommodate the extra length!

Right: *A section of the top surface of the cabinet is on runners so that it can slide back and forth to reveal or conceal the kitchen sink, which forms part of a stainless-steel counter, and the hob.*

Mobile Furniture

Below: *One versatile TV storage solution is to house everything in a unit on castors so that you can move it from place to place as needed. This unit also incorporates boxes to store DVDs and a shelf for books and magazines, all without taking up extra floor space.*

Living in a small home is much more comfortable when movement around the space is unimpeded. Mobile furniture can help you achieve that. What could be better than to be able to whizz bulky furniture out of the way when you don't need it? Fittings that are plumbed in or attached to gas pipes clearly are not candidates for mobility, but if a piece of furniture is on castors, or has the potential for having sturdy lockable castors fitted, then you are in business. Just remember, though, that you must have somewhere to move the piece to!

OFF-THE-PEG OPTIONS

Manufacturers today offer a stylish range of mobile furniture, from simple trolleys, tables and drawer units to modular storage units.

Trolleys and tables

A metal trolley or butcher's block on lockable castors makes a useful extra work surface in the kitchen and you can use the lower shelves for crockery and cutlery. Or use a trolley as a mobile office that you can push out of sight when work is done. Many trolleys are more attractive than mobile work stations from an office supplier. Alternatively, stand the TV on top; that way you can watch in the living area or bedroom as the fancy takes you.

If you need somewhere to perch a laptop, a small table on castors might be perfect. When you are done, move it to your entertaining or sleeping space and you will have somewhere to put your drink or bedtime reading.

Modular and mobile

If you don't mind assembling flatpack furniture, look at modular cube units. You can build the units into the configuration you want and then attach castors to the bottom. Add shelves and doors or leave them open if you want display space. Some versions have brightly coloured doors, which will add a dash of colour to an all-white scheme.

More sophisticated units on lockable castors offer combinations of cupboards, open shelving and pull-out boxes. They may also incorporate a mobile TV stand that you can pull out and use independently of the main combination – providing you unplug the TV first, of course! Some are also suitable for use as a room divider.

BESPOKE UNITS

Unsurprisingly, bespoke mobile furniture offers you the greatest flexibility. Whether you want a mobile office or hanging rail that slides away into a storage wall when not in use, a mobile unit-cum-room divider that accommodates your possessions precisely, or a low bed on castors that pulls out from under a platform, bespoke is the way to go. It offers the ultimate flexibility – your own choice of finish and fixtures, a piece with dimensions that exactly suit your space, and, of course, the chance to own something unique.

Above: *Here, two pine-finished units on lockable castors provide useful extra work surfaces that can be moved around to make a more closed-in kitchen or one that is open to the rest of the living area.*

Left: *This funky green plastic unit is a modern take on the traditional tea trolley.*

Double Up

With space at a premium, why clutter up your already small home with furniture when, with a little ingenuity, you might be able to find one piece that can do the job of two or even three? If you are going down this route, just make sure that what you choose does all its jobs well.

When you are considering multi-function pieces, especially if you are having something made-to-measure, it is important to think carefully about the way you want your whole space to work. There is no point choosing a piece of furniture that combines the functions of sitting and sleeping or sleeping and working if you don't want to do these things in the same part of your home. And before you are seduced by a particularly ingenious design, ask yourself whether, in fact, you actually need a spare bed or a desk area.

The best way of making sure that you have exactly what you want is to buy bespoke. By having a piece designed specially for your space, you could have, for example, a kitchen counter with a hob and oven at one end and an overhang at the other end or along the long edge to provide you with somewhere to sit and eat. Or you might choose banquette-style seating with sturdy drawers built into the backrest. If your budget won't stretch to bespoke, though, there are still plenty of off-the-shelf options to choose from.

SITTING/SLEEPING

Most furniture designed for sitting and sleeping is best reserved for occasional night-time use: as beds, they are often less comfortable than standard. Make sure your space can accommodate your chosen model once it is open.

Sofabeds and sofa chairs

Perhaps the most familiar pieces of dual-purpose furniture are the sofabed and sofa chair: a sofa or chair by day, they open up into a bed by night. Both come in a large variety of styles and fabrics and at a wide range of price points, so you should be able to find one to suit, but check before buying that the opening mechanism works efficiently and is easy to use. Some contemporary versions of the sofabed come as an L-shaped unit. The return has a hinged lid with room beneath for storage. As a variation on the sofa chair, there are also ottomans that open out into a single bed.

The classic sofabed or sofa chair needs space in front to open, but there are also designs for single beds on a metal base whose arms can be lowered, Knole-sofa style. These need extra space at either end. There is even a sofa that converts into bunk beds.

Futons

Japanese-inspired futons, available in single or double versions, are another option, though not everyone finds them comfortable to sleep on. The futons themselves can be heavy to lift and the bases, too, are heavy as well as bulky, which means that they can look overwhelming in a small room. The simplest types are folded onto a hinged slatted wooden base. You lift off the futon, unfold the wooden base and put the unfolded futon in position.

There are also futons on a hinged metal base. The backrest slides backwards so the entire base lies flat with the futon on top. More sophisticated and expensive models promise one-handed opening mechanisms. These are usually more bulky looking and more 'sofa-like'.

Opposite: In a bedroom with an en-suite bathroom, a bespoke unit made from mahogany-coloured MDF serves as both a headboard and a washstand. It even has shelving below for baskets to hold toiletries.

Wall beds

Far more sophisticated is the wall bed that converts into a sofa with shelves above. One single movement brings the shelves down to form a support for the end of the bed – and you do not even have to remove anything from the shelves! Or there is the wall bed that converts into a sofa that you can close away completely if required, leaving just a front panel on view and the whole of the floor space free.

SLEEPING/WORKING

Try a neat wall bed unit with a desk attached. The desk automatically folds down under the double bed base when you open the bed, which is suitable for regular use. A simpler version of this is a metal frame with a shelf on top. The shelf acts as the office space and, when needed, the single or small double bed folds out from underneath, without the need for the shelf to move. More sophisticated versions incorporate storage at either side of the bed.

SLEEPING/STORING

Choose a bed with storage drawers beneath, or a more upmarket version of the same idea, an ottoman-style bed that hinges up, thanks to a gas-pump mechanism, to reveal storage space. Wooden base panels keep stored items off the floor and dust-free, and the bed base takes any type of mattress, as well as a headboard if you wish.

SITTING/STORING

The classic sitting/storage combination is a windowseat. The padded seat hinges upwards revealing storage space below. A variation is the ottoman, which has recently made a comeback.

Right: *This made-to-measure headboard in wenge wood is not only tall enough to act as a divider between the bathroom and the sleeping area, but is also deep enough to incorporate some useful shelves and drawers.*

Designers love the challenge of designing dual-purpose furniture, so there are plenty of unusual dual-purpose combinations to be found. Many are mass-produced, but others are designer pieces with price tags to match. Perhaps one of these will do the job you require, save you space and look good into the bargain.

- The coffee table that lifts up and swivels to become a dining table.

- The bed that houses a TV in the footboard.

- The sofa that incorporates speakers.

- The coffee table that is also a magazine holder.

- The side table whose glass lid swivels to reveal bottle storage beneath.

- The standard lamp that is also an étagère.

- The shower in moulded plastic that is also a bath.

- The headboard that is also a room divider and shelf unit.

- The coffee table that lifts up to reveal a tray underneath.

- The shower that is also a steam cabin.

- The hob that has a fold-down work top.

- The table that converts to a storage chest.

- The chair that converts to a step stool.

- The lamp that is also a bedside table.

- The bookshelf that is also a pair of speakers.

- The magazine stand that doubles as a low table.

- The bed that rolls up and can also be used as a seat, footstool or coffee table.

- The chair that is also an electric hob and work surface.

- The table that is also a sofa.

- The coat rack that is also a bench.

- The wall table that is also a poster frame.

- The door that is also a bookshelf.

- The storage unit that swivels to reveal your flat-screen TV.

- The modernist storage cabinet that is also a safe, complete with a bluetooth–enabled fingerprint-reading lock.

Useful Addresses

GENERAL FURNISHINGS

After Noah
www.afternoah.com
Various branches: retro and antique trolleys, hall storage furniture, extending and drop-leaf tables.

Aram Designs
110 Drury Lane
London WC2B 5SG
020 7557 7557
www.aram.co.uk
Contemporary office furniture, extending and glass tables, storage systems, stacking beds, screens, trolleys.

Authentics
20 High St
Weybridge
Surrey KT13 8AB
01932 871305
www.authentics.co.uk
Bathroom and general storage furniture and accessories.

B & B Italia
www.bebitalia.it
Various branches: contemporary living, dining and bedroom storage furniture, beds with storage beneath.

B & Q
Portswood House
1 Hampshire Corporate Park
Chandlers Ford
Eastleigh SO53 3YX
0845 609 6688
www.diy.com
Various branches: kitchen storage and appliances, sanitary ware, bedroom storage furniture.

BoConcept
www.boconcept.com
Various branches: contemporary storage furniture, extending tables, sofabeds.

Cadira
233–235 Sandycombe Road
Kew
Richmond TW9 2EW
020 8334 1086
www.contemporary-furniture-cadira.co.uk
Contemporary storage furniture, extending tables, beds and coffee tables with storage beneath.

Chaplins
477–507 Uxbridge Road
Hatch End
Pinner HA5 4JS
020 8421 1779
www.chaplins.co.uk
Contemporary designer storage furniture, extending tables, mobile furniture.

Charles Page
61 Fairfax Road
London NW6 4EE
020 7328 9851
www.charlespage.co.uk
Contemporary designer storage furniture, extending and glass tables.

Connections Interiors Ltd
286–288 Leigh Road
Leigh-on-Sea
Essex SS9 1BW
01702 470939
www.connections.uk.net
Contemporary designer storage and mobile furniture, stacking chairs, extending and folding tables, beds with storage beneath.

The Conran Shop
Michelin House
81 Fulham Road
London SW3 6RD
020 7589 7401
www.conran.com
Contemporary, classic, vintage and ethnic furniture.

The Cotswold Company
1 Apollo Rise
Southwood
Farnborough GU14 0GT
01252 391401
www.cotswoldco.com
Traditional-style storage furniture.

Design Icons Ltd
The Coach House
Holly Street
Leamington Spa CV32 4TN
0845 241 3500
www.designicons.co.uk
Contemporary and modern classic furniture, including tables, screens, stacking chairs.

Distinction Furniture and Interiors
Bishops Park House
25–29 Fulham High Street
London SW6 3JH
020 7731 3460
www.distinction-furniture.co.uk
Contemporary storage furniture, glass tables, beds with storage beneath, extending tables.

Dwell
www.dwell.co.uk
Contemporary storage furniture, beds with storage beneath, glass and extending tables, folding and stacking chairs, mobile furniture.

egamma
Wabblegate Farm
Blackgate Lane
Lee Place
Pulborough
West Sussex RH20 1DF
Tel: 0870 1644 201
www.egamma.co.uk
Contemporary stacking chairs, glass coffee tables, nesting tables, gateleg tables.

Furniture Craft International Ltd
Edgware Road
Colindale
London NW9 5AE
Tel: 0870 770 1080
www.fci.uk.com
Contemporary storage furniture, glass tables, stacking chairs, beds with storage beneath.

Habitat
www.habitat.net
Various branches: contemporary storage furniture; nesting, extending, folding and glass tables; stacking and folding chairs; trolleys.

Heal's
The Heal's Building
196 Tottenham Court Road
London W1T 7LQ
020 7636 1666
www.heals.co.uk
Contemporary storage furniture; stacking beds; extending, nesting and glass tables; stacking chairs; trolleys.

The Holding Company
241–245 Kings Road
London SW3 5EL
020 7352 1600
www.theholdingcompany.co.uk
Storage accessories, hall and bedroom storage furniture, trolleys, zinc-fronted cabinets.

Ikea
www.ikea.com
Various branches: contemporary furniture, including storage furniture and accessories, kitchens and kitchen appliances.

John Lewis
www.johnlewis.com
Various branches: stacking and sofabeds; storage furniture and accessories; folding and stacking chairs; folding, extending, glass and nesting tables; kitchen appliances; freestanding modular kitchen units; trolleys.

Kingcome Sofas
114 Fulham Road
London SW3 6HU
020 7244 7747
www.kingcomesofas.co.uk
sofabeds, ottomans.

Laura Ashley
0871 9835 999
www.lauraashley.com
Various branches: traditional and classic storage furniture, nesting and extending tables, mirrored furniture, stacking beds, extending tables.

Ligne Roset
www.ligne-roset.co.uk
Various branches: contemporary sofabeds, glass occasional tables, mobile and storage furniture, stacking chairs, glass and extending tables.

Purves & Purves
020 8838 0200
www.purves.co.uk
Contemporary furniture, including Philippe Starck's Ghost range, plus stacking chairs, glass occasional tables, dining room storage furniture, silver-finished furniture.

SQ2 Living Space
16 Parson Street
London NW4 1QB
020 8203 2122
www.sq2livingspace.co.uk
Fitted and modular furniture for the home office, compact and multi-functional furniture.

Vitra
30 Clerkenwell Road
London EC1M 5PG
020 7608 6200
www.vitra.com
Contemporary mobile and modular storage furniture, tables, screens, stacking chairs.

COMPACT KITCHENS

Anson Concise Ltd
1 Eagle Close
Arnold
Nottingham NG5 7FJ
01159 262102
www.ansonconcise.co.uk
Compact kitchens with stainless-steel finish or a furniture feel.

Elfin Kitchens
Unit 3
Taber Place
Witham
Essex CM8 3YP
01376 501333
www.elfinkitchens.co.uk
Compact kitchens with a range of cooking and storage facilities.

John Strand (MK) Ltd
12/22 Herga Road
Wealdstone
Harrow
Middlesex HA3 5AS
020 8930 6006
www.johnstrand-mk.co.uk
Designer range compact kitchens, including the Mini-Kitchen by Electrolux.

SPACE-SAVING BATHROOM FITMENTS

Armitage Shanks
Armitage
Nr Rugby
Staffordshire WS15 4BT
01543 490253
www.armitage-shanks.co.uk

Ideal Standard UK Ltd
The Bathroom Works
National Avenue
Kingston Upon Hull HU5 4HS
01482 346461
www.ideal-standard.co.uk
Award-winning Space range.

Plumbworld
Units 2, 3 and 4
Millennium Court
Enterprise Way
Evesham
Worcs WR11 1GS
www.plumbworld.co.uk
Small baths, basins, bathroom suites available online.

Roca Ltd
Samson Road
Hermitage Industrial Estate
Coalville
Leicestershire LE67 3FP
01530 830080
www.roca-uk.com

WINDOWS, DOORS AND FLOORING

Becker (Sliding Partitions) Ltd
Wemco House
477 Whippendell Road
Watford
Herts WD18 7QY
01923 236906
www.becker.uk.com
Sliding and folding wall systems in wood veneer, melamine or laminate, or glass.

Dorma UK Ltd
Movable Walls Division
Wilbury Way
Hitchin
Herts SG4 0AB
01462 477 600
www.dorma-uk.co.uk
Acoustic, folding and glass walls and automatic door systems.

D R Services
4 Marshgate Business Centre
Parkway
Harlow Business Park
Harlow
Essex CM19 5QP
01279 445277
www.drservices.co.uk
Glass walls, doors and other fittings; some glass furniture.

Lucite International Ltd
Head Office
Queens Gate
Queens Terrace
Southampton SO14 3BP
08702 404620
www.lucitesolutions.com
Plastics, including Perspex in cast and extruded sheet and in various sizes, thicknesses, colours and textures.

Luxcrete Ltd
Premier House
Disraeli Road
Park Royal
London NW10 7BT
020 8965 7292
www.luxcrete.co.uk
Glass-brick walling, floor lights, roof lights, stair-tread panels.

New House Textiles
How Caple Court
How Caple
Hereford HR1 4SX
01989 740684
www.newhousetextiles.com
Vertical and roller blinds.

Pellfold Parthos Ltd
1 The Quadrant
Howarth Road
Maidenhead
Berkshire SL6 1AP
01628 773353
www.designs4space.com
Folding/sliding partitions, room dividers, movable walls, folding doors, mobile glass walls.

Roger Wilde Ltd
Chareau House
1 Miles Street
Oldham OL1 3NW
0161 624 6824
www.rogerwilde.com
Glass block installation and LITEFLOOR glass flooring.

Rufflette Ltd
Sharston Road
Manchester M22 4TH
0161 998 1811
www.rufflette.com
Panel tracks, custom-made blinds.

Salt
116 OXO Tower
Bargehouse Street
London SE1 9PH
020 7593 0007
www.salt-uk.com
Custom-made sliding panels and roman blinds in unusual contemporary materials.

Sanderson
Chalfont House
Oxford Road
Denham
Middlesex UB9 4DX
01895 830044
www.sanderson-uk.com
Made-to-measure blinds.

Shy UK
1 Bilton Road Industrial Estate
Cadwell Lane
Hitchin

Herts SG4 0SB
Tel: 0845 6720 000
www.shy.co.uk
Electrically operated roller blinds.

Surface Material Design
17 Skiffington Close
London SW2 3UL
020 8671 3383
www.surfacematerialdesign.co.uk
Adhesive film for windows.

Velux Company Ltd
Woodside Way
Glenrothes
Fife KV7 4ND
www.velux.co.uk
Roof windows, sun tunnels, flat roof systems, blinds.

SPACE-SAVING BEDS

Bonbon Trading Ltd
64 Knightsbridge
London SW1X 7JF
0207 352 5202
www.bonbon.co.uk
Wallbeds, storage beds, inflatable beds, sofabeds.

County Beds and Bedrooms
Unit 1B
Denvale Trade Park
Haslett Avenue East
Crawley RH10 1SS
01293 526660
www.countybeds.com
sofabeds, stacking beds.

Deep Surface
Suite 402 + 404, Portland House
Southwell Business Park
Portland
Dorset DT5 2JS
01305 861060
www.deepsurface.co.uk
The Spacia bed that folds away into a floor cavity and the Roller bed that rolls out from a table.

Encompassco
The Pool Room
Stansted House
Stansted Park
Rowlands Castle
Hants PO9 6DX
02392 410045
www.encompassco.com
Sellex shelf beds and Literal wall beds, designed by Lievore-Altherr-Molina.

Litvinoff & Fawcett
281 Hackney Road
London E2 8NA
020 7739 3480
www.landf.co.uk
Bunk beds, stacking beds.

Murphy Wall Beds UK
94 Great South West Road
Hounslow
Middlesex TW4 7NF
020 8572 4188
www.murphywallbeds.co.uk
The original Murphy Wallbed.

The London Wallbed Company
430 Chiswick High Road
Chiswick
London W4 5TF
020 8742 8200
www.wallbed.co.uk
All types of wallbeds.

The Wallbed Workshop
290 Battersea Park Road
London SW11 3BT
020 7924 5300
www.thewallbedworkshop.co.uk
Wide variety of bed conversions and folding and foldaway beds.

Wallbeds Direct
Suite 224
Second floor
The Linen Hall
162/168 Regent Street
London W1B 5TG

020 7434 2066
www.wallbeds-direct.com
All-steel single and double Vertical Wentelbeds®, cupboard surrounds, matching furniture and shelving.

GENERAL CONTACTS

Association of Plumbing and Heating Contractors
14 Ensign House
Ensign Business Centre
Westwood Way
Coventry CV4 8JA
024 7647 0626
www.aphc.co.uk

Institute of Plumbing and Heating Engineers
www.iphe.org.uk
Various branches around the country.

National Inspection Council for Electrical Installation Contracting
Warwick House
Houghton Hall Park
Houghton Regis
Dunstable
Bedfordshire LU5 5ZX
01582 531000
www.niceic.org.uk

Royal Institute of British Architects (RIBA) Bookshops
www.ribabookshops.com
The latest design-led, architectural books online.

The Bathroom Manufacturers Association
Federation House
Station Road
Stoke-on-Trent ST4 2RT
01782 747123
www.bathroom-association.org

Index

Picture Credits

2 Emmanuel Barbe/Architect: Flora de Gastines; 4 Paul Lepreux/Sophie Thévenet, Caroline Tiné; 5 Mai-Linh/Gaël Reyre; 7 Olivier Amsellem/Architect: Philippe Harden; 8 Mai-Linh; 13 Christoph Kicherer/Marie Kalt; 14 Vincent Leroux/Christine Puech; 15 Vincent Leroux/Jean Oddes, José Postic; 16 Vincent Leroux/Christine Puech; 17 Vincent Leroux/Christine Puech; 18 Olivier Amsellem/David Souffan; 19 Vincent Leroux/Christine Puech; 21 Mai-Linh/Catherine Ardouin; 22 Mai-Linh; 24/25 Gilles de Chabaneix/Catherine Ardouin; 27 Mai-Linh/Christine Puech; 29 Paul Lepreux/Catherine Ardouin, Caroline Tiné; 30–1 Mai-Linh/Catherine Ardouin; 32 Alexis Armanet/David Souffan; 33 Mai-Linh/Catherine Ardouin; 34 Bruno Boissonnet/Catherine Ardouin; 35 Kim Cuc/Muriel Martin; 36 Vincent Leroux/Catherine Ardouin/French architect: Joana Abou Khalil; 37 Emmanuel Barbe/Catherine Ardouin; 39 Eric Flogny/Daniel Rozensztroch; 43 Olivier Amsellem/David Souffan/Architect: Philippe Harden; 44 Olivier Amsellem/David Souffan/Architect: Thomas Kickler; 45 Olivier Amsellem/David Souffan/Architect: Philippe Harden; 46 Philippe Garcia/Catherine Ardouin; 47 Emmanuel Barbe/Catherine Ardouin, Marie Kalt; 48 Mai-Linh/Catherine Ardouin; 49 Louis Gaillard/Pascale Chastres/Alix Chatillon; 50/51 Vincent Leroux/Christine Puech; 52 José Van Riele/Jean Oddes, José Postic; 53 Vincent Leroux/Christine Puech; 54/55 Paul Lepreux/Catherine Ardouin, Caroline Tiné; 56 Laurent Teisseire; 57 José Van Riele/Jean Oddes, José Postic; 58 Olivier Amsellem/David Souffan/Architect: Philippe Harden; 60 Nicolas Tosi/Catherine Ardouin; 62/63 Bénédicte Ausset/Catherine Ardouin/Architect: Francesca Cavazzoca Mazzanti; 64/65 Eric Flogny/Daniel Rozensztroch/Paola Navone for Gervasoni; 66 Emmanuel Barbe/Gaël Reyre; 67 Nicolas Tosi/Catherine Ardouin; 68/69 Mai-Linh/Catherine Ardouin; 73 Emmanuel Barbe/Catherine Ardouin/Interior architect: Valérie Mazerat; 75 Zacharie Bauer/Gaël Reyre, Daniel Rozensztroch; 76 Bruno Boissonnet/Christine Puech/Architect: Charlotte Kalt; 77 Christoph Kicherer/Marie Kalt; 78 Vincent Leroux/Jean Oddes, José Postic; 79 Philippe Garcia; 80 Vincent Leroux/Christine Puech; 82 Mai-Linh/Catherine Ardouin; 83 Olivier Amsellem/David Souffan; 84/85 Eric Flogny/Gaël Reyre; 87 Annabel Elston/Marie Kalt/Journalist and stylist: Ilse Crawford/'bureau de style': Studioilse; 88 Bernard Hermann/Daniel Rozensztroch; 89 Mai-Linh/Catherine Ardouin; 91 Eric Flogny/Daniel Rozensztroch; 92 Alexis Armanet/Catherine Ardouin; 93 Philippe Garcia/Gaël Reyre; 94 Philippe Garcia/Gaël Reyre; 95 top Philippe Garcia/Gaël Reyre; **bottom** Alexis Armanet, Catherine Ardouin; 96/97 Vincent Leroux/Gaël Reyre; 101 Antoine Bootz/Daniel Rozensztroch; 102 Mai-Linh/J-Pascal Billaud, Gaël Reyre/Chez Charlotte Perriand, architect and designer; 104/105 Céline Clanet/David Souffan; 106–7 Bénédicte Ausset/Catherine Ardouin/Architect: Francesca Cavazzoca Mazzanti; 108 Paul Lepreux/Marie Kalt; 109 Olivier Amsellem/David Souffan; 110 Vincent Leroux/Jean Oddes, José Postic; 111 Gilles de Chabaneix/Catherine Ardouin; 112 top Eric Flogny/Daniel Rozensztroch/Damsgard Country Mansion, tel: +47 559 40 870; **bottom** Vincent Leroux/Christine Puech; 113 Bruno Boissonnet/Catherine Ardouin; 114 Paul Lepreux/Catherine Ardouin, Caroline Tiné; 115 Vincent Leroux/Jean Oddes, José Postic; 116 Louis Gaillard; 117 Paul Lepreux/Marie Kalt; 118 left Paul Lepreux/Catherine Ardouin, Caroline Tiné; **right** Mai-Linh/Catherine Ardouin; 119 Philippe Garcia/José Postic, Christine Puech; 120 Mai-Linh/Catherine Ardouin; 121 Vincent Leroux/Christine Puech; 123 Mai-Linh/Catherine Ardouin; 124/125 Vincent Leroux/Christine Puech; 126 Vincent Leroux/Daniel Rozensztroch; 127 Alexis Armanet/David Souffan/Interior architect: Emmanuel Renoird; 128 Pénélope Chauvelot/Michelle Bocquillon; 129 Vincent Leroux/J-Pascal Billaud; 130–1 Alexis Armanet/David Souffan; 132 Alexis Armanet/Catherine Ardouin; 133 Céline Clanet/David Souffan; 134 Paul Lepreux/Marie Kalt; 135 Jacques Caillaut; 139 Bénédicte Ausset/Catherine Ardouin/Architect: Francesca Cavazzoca Mazzanti; 140 Olivier Amsellem/David Souffan; 141 Emmanuel Barbe/Catherine Ardouin; 142 Mai-Linh/J-Pascal Billaud, Gaël Reyre/Chez Charlotte Perriand, architect and designer; 143 Olivier Amsellem/David Souffan/Architect: Philippe Harden; 145 Mai-Linh/Gaël Reyre; 146 Nicolas Tosi/Julie Borgeaud; 147 top Mai-Linh/Catherine Ardouin, Caroline Tiné; **bottom** Marie Pierre Morel/Christine Puech, Gaël Reyre; 148 Christoph Kicherer/Marie Kalt; 150–1 Vincent Leroux/Christine Puech; 152 Vincent Leroux/Jean Oddes, José Postic.